CW00503386

Linc[illegible]
Heritage De[illegible]ctive

An exploratory walk around Lincoln's past

Danny Walsh

SIGMA Leisure

© Danny Walsh, 2017

All Rights Reserved. No part of this publication may be reproduced, stored in a retrieval system, or transmitted in any form or by any means - electronic, mechanical, photocopying, recording, or otherwise - without prior written permission from the publisher or a licence permitting restricted copying issued by the Copyright Licensing Agency, 90 Tottenham Court Road, London W1P 0LA. This book may not be lent, resold, hired out or otherwise disposed of by trade in any form of binding or cover other than that in which it is published, without the prior consent of the publisher.

Moral Rights: The author has asserted his moral right to be indentified as the Author of this Work.

Published by Sigma Leisure - an imprint of
Sigma Press, Stobart House, Pontyclerc, Penybanc Road, Ammanford, Carmarthenshire SA18 3HP.

British Library Cataloguing in Publication Data
A CIP record for this book is available from the British Library.

ISBN: 978-1-910758-26-7

Typesetting and Design by: Sigma Press, Ammanford.

Cover photographs: © Danny Walsh
top (left to right): The High Bridge; Cathedral turret with Bishop Hugh; St George and the Dragon - detail from George III's bust in the castle; Castle Hill Club - A hangman's bed and breakfast.
main image: Cathedral chapter house.

Photographs: © Danny Walsh, unless otherwise stated.

Printed by: Akcent Media Ltd.

Disclaimer: the information in this book is given in good faith and is believed to be correct at the time of publication. No responsibility is accepted by either the author or publisher for errors or omissions, or for any loss or injury howsoever caused. Only you can judge your own fitness, competence and experience. Do not rely solely on sketch maps for navigation: we strongly recommend the use of appropriate Ordnance Survey (or equivalent) maps.

CONTENTS

ACKNOWLEDGEMENTS

The author would like to express his gratitude to the following for giving permission to use photographs taken upon their premises.

The Collection and Usher Gallery, Lincoln. Further credit for some individual items is given in the text.

Lincolnshire County Council Museum of Lincolnshire Life, (and Bovington Museum for permission to photograph the tank).

Cathedral images by kind permission of Lincoln Cathedral.

Otherwise the pictures are taken from the authors collection with some additional photography by Dr David Howard.

INTRODUCTION

This is not a history of Lincoln … but it is a walk which will engage you with what are arguably Lincoln's 'best bits'! However it also takes in oddities and quirks which are often walked past and overlooked even by the locals. The book will take you to places but you will sometimes have to do a little detective work to pinpoint some of the features. On the walk you will encounter much of the history that has shaped this great city and made it what it is. Yates and Thorold (1965) describe the approach to Lincoln from the south with the cathedral 'sailing above you' as 'one of the great sights of Europe'. Most visitors are inclined to agree and are also somewhat surprised, once they have got their breath back, to discover that Lincolnshire is not at flat as they thought.

The Lincoln born distinguished archaeologist and historian Maurice William Barley describes a route through Lincolnshire along the Western escarpment of the limestone edge as 'the Great North Road of prehistoric times' (Barley 1952). Here the river Witham cuts a 'gap' through the limestone ridge that runs up the spine of Lincolnshire and it was here that the Roman Ninth Legion brought Ermine Street north along the scarp and established a temporary camp overlooking the river Witham. This Roman settlement was to become *Lindum Colonia* or Lincoln. The line of this ancient track through Lincoln forms the backbone of our exploration of the city's Heritage. The road passes through magnificent arches and along Bailgate where the old Roman road is now some eighteen or so feet below your feet and the modern street level. At the bottom of the scarp the Romans dug out the Witham to create a pool, the Brayford, an inland harbour bringing access and trade along the Witham from Boston and the North Sea.

THE LINCOLN CIRCLE LINE

W	War Memorial
SM	St Marks Station
BL	Site of the Battle of Lincoln 1911
SML	St Mary Le Wigford Church
C	Cornhill
SB	St Benedicts
HB	High Bridge
BP	Brayford Pool
ML	Much Lane
S	Stonebow
SHC	St Hugh's Chambers
CH	Cardinals Hat
JH	Jews House
H	Harlequin
CHT	Christs Hospital Terrace
CVH	Chad Vara House
AH	Aaron's House
WC	Widow Cullen's
SMM	St Mary Magdalene
LPH	Leigh Pemberton House
CHC	Castle Hill Club
JL	Judges Lodgings
LC	Lincoln Castle
TL	The Lawns
OL	Occupation Lane
MOLL	Museum of Lincolnshire Life
EM	Ellis' Mill
ST	Strugglers
WT	Water Tower
NA	Newport Arch
B	Bailgate
SP	St Paul in the Bail
WH	White Hart
BHC	Black Horse Chambers
DW	Deans Wife
MY	Minster Yard
E	Exchequergate
LCA	Lincoln Cathedral
BP	Bishops Palace
CHO	Chapter House
T	Tennyson Statue
P	Priorygate
PO	Pottergate
GS	Greestone Stairs
UG	Usher Gallery
TC	The Collection
SS	Silver Street
DH	Drill Hall
GF	Grey Friars
SSW	St Swithins
RW	River Witham
M	Market

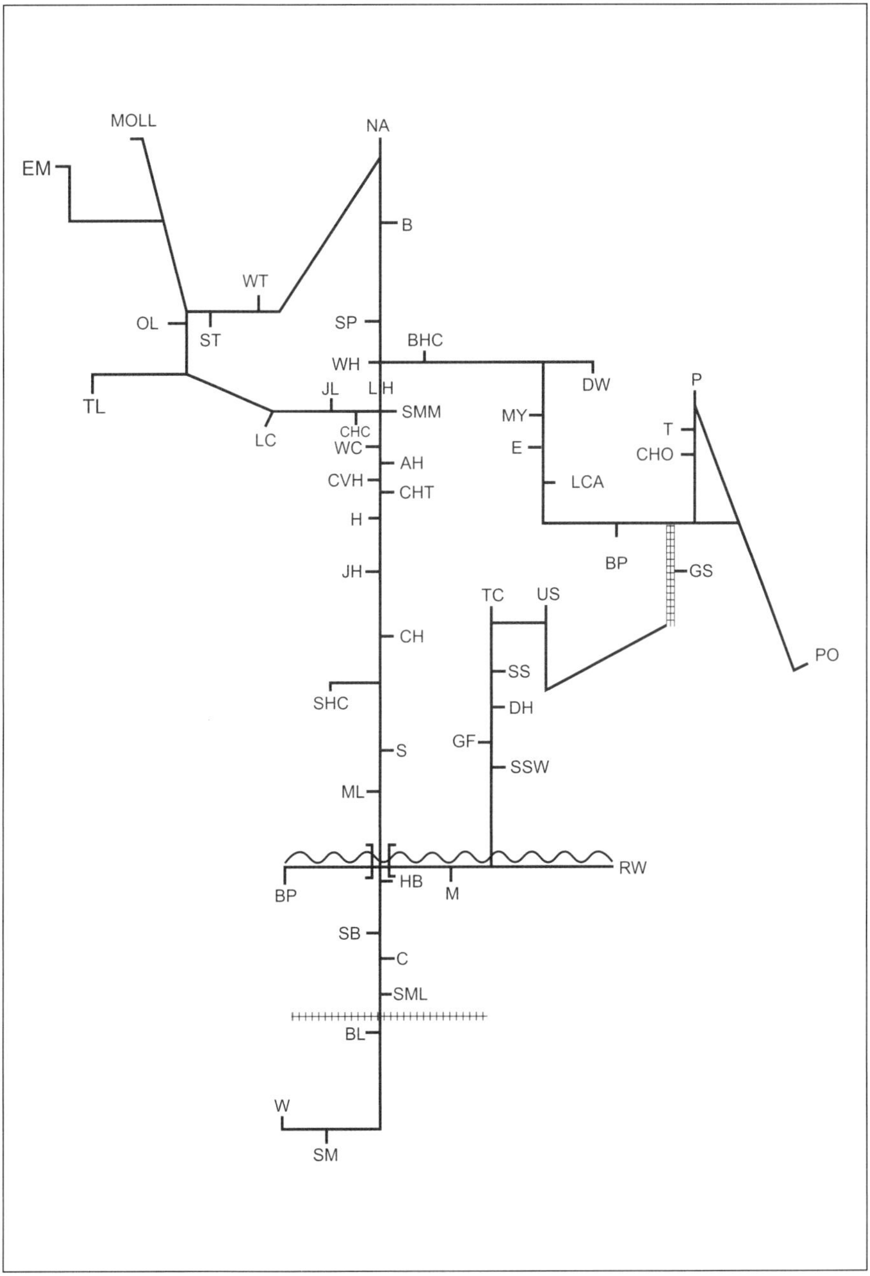
MOLL
NA
EM
B
WT
OL
ST
SP
BHC
WH
TL
JL
L H
SMM
DW
P
MY
T
LC
CHC
WC
E
CHO
AH
LCA
CVH
CHT
H
BP
JH
GS
TC
US
CH
PO
SS
SHC
DH
GF
S
SSW
ML
RW
BP
HB
M
SB
C
SML
BL
W
SM

Lindum means ‘the hill fort by the pool’. ’Dun’ is an ancient word meaning hill fort and ‘llin’ is derived from the Celtic ‘llyn’ or ‘lin’ meaning lake, pool or mere ... So we get ‘Lindum Colonia’ ... the city on the hill above the pool.

Since Roman times Lincoln has added to its heritage with some of the country’s finest architecture. From the Norman Jews House, castle, the crowning glory of the Gothic cathedral, the Tudor houses of Bailgate to the preserved railway engineering sheds of the 21st century university, at every corner there are gems to be seen. The walk covers a lot of heritage in a small area but to do it justice you will need several days if not a week. Morton (1929) aptly sums Lincoln up as ‘a hill sacred to English history’ ... enjoy.

ST MARKS TO THE STONEBOW

St Marks

We begin half way down the High Street at the St Marks shopping area and what used to be Lincolns second railway station. The portico of what is now a shop being the rather grand entrance to the station.

Further into the precinct stands the 'Obelsik'. Built in 1762/3 as a water conduit it was restored in 1863 and

placed on the High Bridge as the 'Albert Fountain' in tribute to the Prince Consort. However it turned out to be too heavy for the bridge and was eventually dismantled, placed in storage then placed here when the area was redeveloped as we see it today.

High Street

Out on the High Street to the south is the aptly named South Common and to the North the tantalising prospect of a walk along Ermine Street and on up to the Cathedral Quarter. Just down the High Street we meet a level crossing which was once the focus of a Lincoln revolt. Unhappy times occurred in Summer 1911 when between the Stonebow and the old St Marks station four days of riots ensued as trades unionists supported striking rail-workers. The chief constable had had the Boiler Makers Union banner torn down during a peaceful demonstration. Then some days later he ordered his policemen to use their truncheons as a group of protestors stopped the rail crossing gates from opening. The signal box was set upon, a train smashed through the gates and a full blown riot ensued.

Site of the battle of Lincoln 1911!

Troops were made ready but stood down only for it to flare up again the next day with St Marks station and the railway offices taking the brunt being set ablaze and gutted. Dr Mansell Sympson stepped up as a magistrate and read the Riot Act backed by the recalled troops who the crowd were told would fire upon them if there was not 'an immediate cessation of disturbances'! Bayonets were drawn and the crowd realised they were beaten.

St Mary le Wigford

Many years ago this area used to be very marshy and was called Wickenford from a Danish word for creek. When William the Conqueror built his castle uphill he demolished 166 houses and it is thought that those poor folk forcibly displaced in the process settled here. An old guide to the church has it that the tower was built around that period as an act of defiance and independence! The two light round headed windows with a central shaft and the quoining (the large corner stones) of the walls are characteristic of work from before the Norman Conquest and this may have been a snub and deliberate act of rebelliousness to maintain the traditional styles.

above*: Quoining;*
top right*: The west door is rounded with 'dog-toothing' as per the Norman style:*
right*: The round headed window*

The church is in fact built over a Roman cemetery and a Roman tombstone is set into the tower by the door. It commemorates Sacer, son of Bruscus, and his wife Carssouna and son Quintus. The stone seems to have been used long after their deaths as a kind of dedication stone for the church for above their inscription is another in Anglo Saxon which roughly translates as 'Eirtig had me built to the glory of God and St Mary'.

above: Roman tombstone, Alice Hall's grave; top right: ...and can you find the grave of the Graves?; right: The conduit

The cemetery below and this important stone remind us that Lincoln was a great Roman fortress and important trading centre. Outside are many old graves and tombs complete with original inscriptions and carvings. See if you can find this fine inscription on the grave of Alice Hall.

Also outside is an interesting conduit. The Greyfriars in Lincoln had laid a conduit or water pipes to supply water to their Friary and when Henry VIII dissolved the Friary in 1538 he gave its water supply to the city. This was very 'generous' of him given the considerable plundering of the treasures of the cathedral he undertook in order to fill his coffers! The water supply was later expanded and pipes were laid to three new conduits one of which is this at St Mary's from which water could be drawn.

Inside the church has much of interest, see if you can find ... the fine Medieval windows in the North aisle (in need of a clean!) ... and this one (*right*).

There are also some fine Victorian windows depicting scenes from the nativity (*below*), and a worn stone

figure of a woman in a recess of the north wall (*above*).

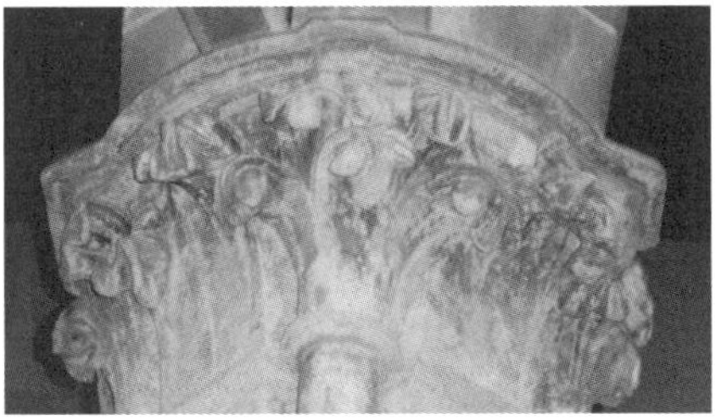

There are Early English pillars with capitals decorated in foliage in the North arcade (*left*).

Some pillars have unusual polygonal concave faces and the bases of the pillars have hollows which some say would hold holy water (*right*).

Note too the Tudor rose on the deeply carved octagonal font (*below*).

There is also brass of 1525 on the West wall of the nave marking the burial place of one John Jobson an alderman and fishmonger with the tools of his trade an axe and fish nife engraved on it (*below*).

Some sources suggest that in 1158 in this church Henry II had his second coronation following his previous one in London. This was not unusual in those times but it was done here instead of the cathedral because superstition had it that it was an ill omen to wear a crown within the walls of the City of Lincoln, and the church was just outside. Maybe the hardest thing to spot is this curious cat face on the bottom of the tomb cover of one of Henry VIII's servants near the door (*right*).

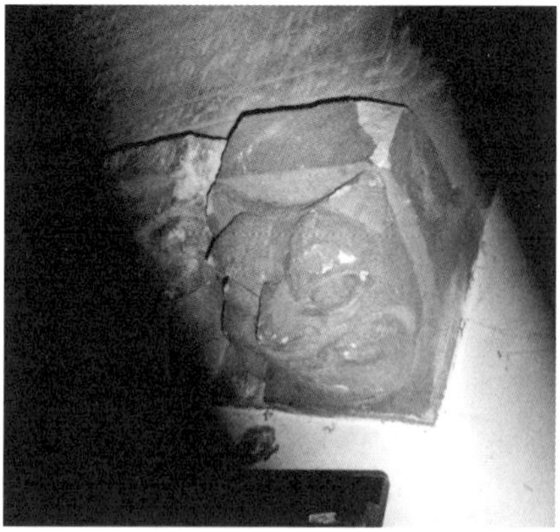

The Nomad trust runs a homeless shelter here and has the fine core value of trying to give people at their lowest ebb a feeling of worth.

High Street

From the reign of Charles II an April horse fair was held in the High Street. On the Monday and Tuesday of the last week of April horses would line the street from the Stonebow to St Mary le Wigfords. As well as horses there would be boxing, jugglers, circus acts, stalls and basically what we would call a fun fair. In the 1930s the fair was moved to the West Common and it died out in the early 1950s a victim of the car. But the annual spring pleasure fair is still a feature of the city calendar being held now on the South Common.

One of the first buildings you will come across is this fine example of terracotta work (*below*).

It was designed in 1897 by Edwardian Lincoln architect William Watkins as Peacock Wilson's Bank and has subsequently been used as several different shops.

Terracotta coat of arms. The horse is a symbol of readiness to serve King and Country

The building comes complete with its own pigeon protectors

There is a marked contrast with more modern architecture opposite .... apparently this was designed!

Watchmakers James Usher and Sons worked out of 192 High Street. His son was to gift the city its art gallery. This was also the first business and shop in Lincoln to have electricity which he generated himself! (*top right*)

Over the road note the Black Swan one of Lincoln's many lost pubs (*right*).

Cornhill

Half way up the High Street you will find the Cornhill. This was built upon the burial ground of the former church of St John the Evangelist. A market for grain was first held here in 1598 but it was not until 1848 that the Corn Exchange itself was built. Here too were held flourishing markets selling poultry, farm implements, tools, vegetables and basically anything under the sun from seafood to second hand clothes. Boisterous auctions were held and

The impressive Corn Exchange frontage

street entertainers of the strong man variety plied their trade amongst many a quack doctor and con man.

The Corn Exchange ultimately proved to be too small and a new one was built adjacent in 1897 which now houses the City's Market (*right*).

Back on the high street ... it is important to look up above the shop windows and take in some of the splendid architecture. If only we had kept it all the way down to street level!

Leaving Cornhill note the Capital and Counties Bank Limited frieze over the Lloyds doorway. Lloyds took it over in 1918 (*lower right*).

Many of these buildings used to be pubs or coaching inns. So over the road note Laura Ashley with its fine corbels (*left*) as this used to be the much loved Roebuck pub.

St Benedicts church

This is said to have been the richest church in the city attended by wealthy merchants in the Middle Ages. It is a 13/14th century replacement for what was a Saxon church on this site. It was severely damaged in the Civil War and restored in 1932. The tower retains the familiar Saxon style belfry windows (*below*).

The church has its back to the high street but represents the best tea and biscuits in town, It provides a welcome respite from the fury of Saturday shopping. Note the medieval window with modern letter box! And the larger window to the rear (*below*).

Also the stone coffins in the garden and some interesting faces along the gutter line (*below*).

Inside are a central pillar with capitals of overhanging leaves, and an old pulpit. There is also an old brass of Alderman John Becke, two times mayor and his seven sons, his wife and two daughters wearing wide brimmed hats and in the folds of the mothers gown is a maid holding a skull! (*right*)

Be sure to notice this nice statue too (*left*) ... and the monument of a Lady who became immortal! (*below*)

And is this a lion? (*right*)

The church once had a curfew bell called 'Old Kate', ringing in the morning at six to summon people to work and again at seven in the evening to tell them to go home. It is said that it also rang later to let people know it was time to snuff the candles and put out their lamps.

The War Memorial

The city's war memorial (*left*) is in front of the church and it is a pleasant spot to sit and watch the world go by and a favourite spot for the city's many talented buskers as well as others of a more dubious musical ability. Look for these angels...

This area was known as St Benedicts Square and Lincoln's first public transport was a horse drawn tram from here to Bracebridge on the outskirts. It took 20 minutes and cost 2d. The horses were replaced by an electric tramway in 1905 and

apparently the trams only shaved 5 minutes off the horse's time. In the 1920s motor buses took over. Opposite the war memorial at 305/6 high street is a marvellous piece of building work. This ornate brick and terracotta façade was designed by William Watkins and built in 1900. It was built for the company of Hewitt Brown and note the HB in the shield above the top window and the side chimney stacks (*left*).

Just before the High Bridge notice the purpose built Marks and Spencers store, and it's M and S logo! (*below*)

High Bridge

High bridge marks the spot where the Roman Ermine Street forded the River Witham. The Norman bridge here was constructed around 1160. This treasure of the 12th century is the oldest medieval bridge in the country to still have buildings upon it. It was restored in 1901 when it was stripped back to its timber frame and you could look right through it! It was faithfully returned to its half-timbered shops three stories high.

This is what it used to look like

The bridge used to have houses on either side and many must have walked over it never knowing that it was bridge. Opposite the Tudor buildings, on the east side of the bridge, there used to be a small chapel of St Thomas, sadly no longer. In 1549 the bells were removed and it was converted into a house but this was pulled down around 1763 and an obelisk erected in its place. This eventually became too heavy for the bridge and was removed to the new St Marks shopping precinct at Lincolns old St Marks railway station.

Today the old and the new are tastefully interwoven and the High Bridge is a good place to sit and watch the world go by.

On the bridge stands Stokes coffee shop where Robert William Stokes has ground and sold coffee for many years. Since about 1910 he had a coffee shop called the Arcadia Café just down the road which he sold to Marks and Spencer, then in 1937 he bought the half-timbered shop on the bridge we now know as 'Stokes'. He died in 1951 but the business flourishes and is now part of Lincoln's heritage (*left*).

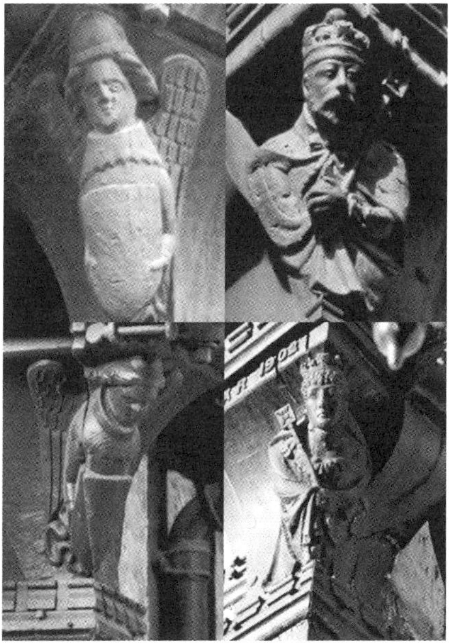

Note these carvings of angels and kings on the angle brackets at the corners of the building

The view of the Witham from the top floor of Stokes coffee shop

Brayford Pool

The steps on either side of Stokes take you down towards the Brayford and show the Witham sliding through the dark narrow arch locally called the 'Glory Hole' but in past times known as the 'murder hole'! (*left*)

Bodies dropped into the Brayford would get stuck here against the bridge sides as the river narrowed to get under the arch. Around 1842 there used to be a pub down here called the 'Rose in June' and it is suggested that 'dodgy' goings on relating to the pub are the origin for these suggestive names. Sneak down

the steps and take a quick look at the Brayford. You can walk down one side and come back up the other.

Where the Witham cuts through the limestone of the Lincoln Edge pools were formed and the largest was known as Bradeford or Broad ford. This was a marshy area but the Romans realised its potential and dug it out to create an inland port albeit 40 miles from the sea! They then dug the Fosse Dyke linking the Witham to the Trent so you could sail from the Wash and Boston, up the Witham to the Brayford, out along the Foss to the Trent and from here on up to York, via the Ouse, or along the Humber and down to the Wash and back round again. Just along the Witham from the Brayford another Roman canal the Carr Dyke ran south to join the Nene at Peterborough. The canal was used to supply the Roman legions and camps with corn from the fens. These were the only Roman canals in Britain and are as important as Hadrian's Wall. Objects considered to be votive gifts have been found in the Witham around Lincoln, such as the bronze Witham Shield dating back to the Iron Age around 400BC. The original is now in the British Museum. It is worth walking along the bank a little to get the view back of the cathedral across the water (*below*).

Because of the Brayford and the waterways Lincoln flourished in the Middle Ages with trade in wool and wool cloth especially the famous Lincoln Green and Scarlet. Try to imagine this view of the cathedral as it would have looked in the 18th and 19th centuries at the height of the Industrial Revolution. The pool would have been surrounded by massive warehouses, granaries, mills, pubs, coal and timber yards and at the many wharves would be huge sailing barges tied up ready for hauling grain and timber. There was even an iron steam passenger boat plying between Lincoln and Boston.

The view, as was, from an old postcard

The coming of the railways, which could move goods and people cheaper, heralded the decline of the 'port' but it was busy until the early 20th century. From then it declined rapidly and decayed with derelict warehouses and sunken barges combining to make a forlorn sight. In 1964 it was nearly filled in to create a car park but common sense prevailed, the Brayford Trust was set up and it was developed into the marina we see today. This busy leisure area is the focus for many craft fairs, food markets, and festivals including the annual Waterside Festival and a

wonderful location for the city's ever growing University.

Coming back to the High Street the view of the rear and underneath High Bridge is a fine sight when filled with flotillas of the towns many Mute Swans which used to be requisitioned to supply the royal banquets of Henry VIII (*bottom of previous page*).

Back on the high street note the ornate architecture at the corner of the Waterside centre (*left*).

Then look out for this …

You have probably just walked past it … not *much* notice gets taken of it!

The George Inn stood on the corner of High St and Guildhall St (now HSBC) next to the Stonebow. Almost opposite on the High St was the Saracens Head. Both were coaching inns in the golden age of coaching when it would take about 15 hours to get to London and cost the equivalent of around £1.50. You can still see the wrought iron balcony of the Saracens Head (*left*).

The building is still put to good use as Waterstones booksellers but it would be nice to walk in and see the books surrounded by Victoriana, aspidistras and a Victorian bar!

The Spread Eagle next door was another but this became Woolworths and now is the Waterside Centre. When James I visited in 1617 it is said he watched a cock fight in the George then went to the Spread Eagle to watch a local take on a court attendant in a fencing match, needless to say the Lincoln man won! The Saracens head didn't close until 1959. Older locals will recall being able to buy bags of mixed of biscuits chosen from open tins at 'Woolies' then pop next door to Mac Fisheries for their fresh fish.

How times change! ... When this was built what lies underneath would raise a few eyebrows!

Opposite is a city coat of arms atop the Midland bank (*left*).

The Stonebow

The name 'Stonebow' comes from 'stennibogi', a Norse word meaning stone arch. Spanning Ermine Street this was the site of the Roman South Gate which fell into disrepair, was demolished and then rebuilt as the southern gate of the medieval city. Around 1237 the Guildhall was moved to rooms over the arch. Here were held Mayoral banquets, the food for which was supplied by the cities tenants! Richard II visited the city in 1387 and gave the Mayor the right of having a sword borne before him and gave him his own royal sword which is still here in the treasury. The Medieval gateway was also by now in poor repair and Richard ordered a new one to be built. The funds were squandered and it was to take over a hundred years for the new one to be built finally completing in 1520. It was built by William Spencer a freemason of the city. Standing here you are in good company as Henry VIII, Catherine of Aragon, James I and Richard II have all passed under its arches. It is hard to believe that traffic flowed through it and on down the High Street until 1973.

Saltergate used to be called prison lane as from 1586 the Stonebow became the main city prison. This was convenient with the court in the Guildhall above. In the east wing, rooms were used as a debtor's prison, one for men

This old view is charming but the building beyond Pratt and Sons has long gone

and one for women. The lower damp earth dungeons were for common criminals. There was no exercise yard, no water and no straw and Abell and Chambers (1939) tell us that to add insult to injury when they were released debtors had to pay the gaolers a fee of 6s and 8d! Apparently the debtors rooms had small iron grated windows at pavement level giving the prisoners glimpses of the feet of passers by. This allowed friends and family to see and talk to them through the gratings and also to pass in food and drink. The drink was often alcohol so that according to Abell and Chambers a visitor in 1802 found them to be half starved, and suffocated ... but intoxicated. They called the prison one of the worst in the kingdom and a disgrace to the city and shocking to humanity. The gaol was abandoned in 1809 pulled down in 1842 and the whole wing was rebuilt in similar stone to the rest of the Stonebow (*right*).

The second floor is now the Guildhall and used as the council chamber. Lincoln's council meet here under its oak beams. Looking up from the south and to the right you can see the mote bell dating from 1371. It is still used to call councillors to meetings and is the oldest such bell in England. Inside next to a portrait of King George III is a 'Willis' medal with the inscription 'Britons rejoice, your King's restored'. The other face has a portrait of Dr Francis Willis who cured the King's Madness! (See the 'Lawns' section). What used to be the old debtors prison is now the guildhall treasury which houses a variety of historic civic treasures, including the sword given by Richard II and the city regalia such as the Mayors chain of office and 'posy' ring, which marries the mayor to the city! The clock on both sides dates from 1888 and is used by locals to fool visitors who are advised to meet them on the 'clock side'!

The Stonebow was also traditionally where locals would see the New Year in but these days a larger gathering occurs in Castle Square and in front of the cathedral.

Look out for the following ... St Mary, Patron Saint of Lincoln (*below left*).

She is portrayed in prayer standing on a serpent the symbol of evil (*below*).

On her left is arch angel Gabriel holding a palm and a scroll (*far right*).

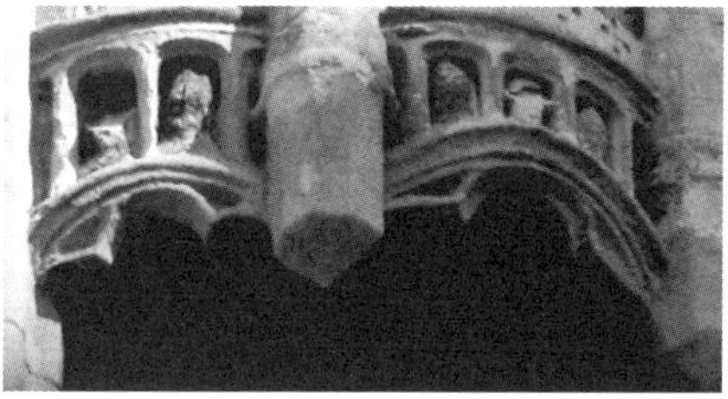

Above Gabriel's head ... are these little people looking out of a gallery! (*below*) The coat of arms is James 1 added in 1617 to commemorate his visit (*right*).

There is also a Lincoln coat of arms (*right*).

But be sure to look at all the corbel heads, grotesques and strange creatures on the face of the Stonebow (*below*).

There's also a Tudor rose and a Fleur de Lys, and see if you can spot this 'pig'! (*below*)

THE STONEBOW TO CASTLE SQUARE

Just past the Stonebow note the old Smiths Bank sign (*right*), and over the crossing another city shield (*below left*).

Further up the road look out for this pleasing art deco feature above the shop fronts (*left*).

Before you cross the next crossing just turn left into Corporation Street and take note of St Hugh's Chambers built in 1899 as the offices for a firm of solicitors. The central door shield and rampant lions are topped with some wonderful white relief griffins on a pale bluer background (*next page*).

And over the next crossing guess what shop this was! (*right*)

And note the stone initials and scallop (*below*).

A little further up on the left you will find these classical lines … (*left*)

Cardinals Hat and Dernstall House

These are fine examples of half-timbered Tudor houses. The Cardinals Hat is named after Cardinal Thomas Wolsey who was the Dean and later Bishop of Lincoln from 1514.

This building was originally an inn dating from the late 1400s. Like many Tudor buildings, the upper floors lean out over the lower floor. In Elizabethan times property taxes related to the ground space, or footprint, the building took up. So to pay less but maximise the floor space upper floors overhung those below often leading to dark streets (*right*).

If you slip down the side alley you'll find this monkey over the door (*below*). It has recently been restored as a pub allowing you to see the Medieval architecture inside as well as sample some local beer,

Next door Dernstall House is late 15th century and whilst it is less imposing than the Cardinals Hat it contains masonry dating from the 12th century. The surrounding area was called Dernstall in medieval times and was thought to be a Jewish area, second in size only to London.

This pair of timber framed historic buildings stand at the start of 'The Strait' section of Lincoln's Steep Hill.

The Strait

On your way up the hill see if you can spot this representation of the Lincoln Imp (*right*).

Jews House

Arguably this is one of the country's finest examples of Norman domestic architecture. It was built around 1170 at a time when few houses were built of stone. The house gets its name from the Jewess Belaset who once lived here and was hanged in 1290 for 'clipping' the King's coin. The Norman town house has a fine carved Norman archway with a cable interlacing

pattern and there are traces of pillars with foliage capitals too (*below*). Note also the chimney flue above the door then cross the road and look back at the fine arched windows on the first floor (*right*).

From the doorway is a passage leading to store rooms and work-shops and steps up to the living quarters on the first floor which is why the fire place is above the door. The ground floor didn't have windows at that time just slits as a protective measure from thieves and to safeguard the goods inside. When built it would have been one room thick from front to back. Twelfth century stone houses are rare and only the wealthy could afford them. Belaset was a money lender and would have been grateful for the protection the stone gave her.

Jews Court

This Norman town house next door to the Jews House is believed to have once been a synagogue (*right*).

It was called 'court' after a supposed mock trial which led to a gruesome crucifixion. In 1255 a boy named Hugh disappeared in the Dernstall area at the bottom of Steep Hill. He was last seen playing with some Jewish children at the house of a Jew named Copin. Local legend suggests he was lured inside and murdered. According to E Mansell Sympson (1906) the Jews stole a child for a sacrifice and summoned Jews from cities across England to take part. A Lincoln Jew was appointed judge in the place of Pilate and the boy was beaten and mocked being called 'Jesus the false prophet' and made to wear a crown of thorns before being crucified. His mother who had been looking for him went into Copin's house and discovered the body of a child in a well. According to Abell and Chambers (1939) Copin said that when they tried to bury the body 'the earth vomited it forth' so they put it down the well. On hearing the story the cathedral canons took possession of the body and the boy was henceforth regarded as a martyr. They buried him with honour in the cathedral. Some years later it was suggested that the well was the one in Jews Court but this has been discredited. 'Little Hugh' however did exist and he had a shrine in the cathedral which was opened up in 1791 by the Dean and Sir Joseph Banks where they found a pickled childs skeleton. Legend has it that Banks tasted the pickle fluid!

The tale continues and relates to the general persecution of the Jews at that time. Copin had been promised his life if he confessed but this promise was broken and he was tied to a horse's tail and dragged through town and hung on Canwick Hill. The whole affair led to unsound trials, with many Jews accused and witnesses tortured. 91 other Jews were arrested and sent to London for trial where all were sentenced to death! One rationale for this persecution is that many had a vested interest in the Jews being found guilty. Those who had borrowed money would naturally seek an easy chance to scapegoat those whom they owed money to. Upon their deaths according to the law the king would inherit all a Jews wealth and possessions and those who owed them money would have their debts wiped out! Today Jews Court houses the Society for Lincolnshire History and Archaeology and its bookshop. See www.slha.org.uk for a treasure house of local history and a testament to the excellent work of local historians.

The open space outside Jews Court was at one time used for bull baiting with Danes Terrace opposite at one time being called Bull Ring Lane. The other lane leading out of the square is called Well Lane after the legend. Well Lane is a far easier gradient that the Romans would have used to zig zag their carts up the hill.

Note the old water pump with the coat of arms ... but its when you get to the top that you'll be needing the drink! So now for a bit of exercise!

Steep Hill

H V Morton (1929) calls this an 'abrupt hill' adding that 'the hill is so steep that you clamber up to the cathedral grasping an iron handrail; and it is no ordinary task!' In 1732 the Mayor erected a bench half way up where the hill meets Danesgate much to the gratitude of the modern tourist who mistakenly thought Lincolnshire was flat.

A local pastime is watching tourists discover this is not the case as they try to get their breath back on the way to the cathedral. The clue is in the name! The spot is still known as the Mayors Chair. The railings behind were originally to stop any foolish person trying to take a horse and cart or carriage down the hill!

Harlequin

This excellent 16th century antiquarian bookshop used to be an inn much frequented by actors and artistes appearing at the theatre back down the hill. It is a welcome place to

browse whilst you calm your lungs down.

Christs Hospital Terrace

This corner is usually bypassed but is worthy of note. This Victorian church of St Michael on the Mount replaced a nearby medieval one which was sacked by Parliamentarians in the civil war. A new church was started in 1854 to accommodate the growing parish and number of boys at the nearby Christ's Hospital or 'Bluecoat' school. It was finished in 1871 and made redundant in 1998. It is a quirky Gothic design by Tuelon and note especially the bell tower. Sadly now it is a private residence. However the old bluecoat school of the Christs Hospital Trust remains. It was founded in 1612 and was a charitable trust originally taking twelve boys and educating them until the age of 16 preparing them for trades and apprenticeships. The current building dates from 1784.

The school closed in 1833 and the money from it was used to build the Christs Hospital School for Girls which we later pass down Greestone Steps. After its closure it was at one time the Lincoln College of Art.

Aaron the Jews House or Norman House

This Medieval house is reputed to be the oldest inhabited stone dwelling house in England. Dating from around 1170 it was thought to have once been the home of Aaron, a wealthy Jewish money lender. This is now disputed but the house is still associated with him. The round arched doorway had a corbelled chimney shaft over it which is now a window.

The first floor has a complete double arched window finely restored in 1878 and is how many Norman windows would have looked (*left*).

The walls are 3 to 4 foot thick and the only windows downstairs would have been slits as the houses of money lenders were apt to be mobbed and robbed. Without Aaron's loans Lincoln cathedral could not have been built. Some suggest he was the wealthiest man in Norman Britain! He funded 16 cathedrals and abbeys in all and his loans to Henry II were half the Kings income! The Jews were unpopular because of the heavy rate of interest they charged and at the time Christians were not allowed to practice usury and receive any interest thus when money was needed it was to the Jews people turned. Upon Aaron's death Henry II seized his estate and thus wiped out a considerable personal and national debt! Look for this poor chap seemingly holding up the arch.

Nearby on opposite sides of the street are boundary stones marking the boundary between the castle Constable's patch and the city council. City folk had to be out of the castle grounds before sunset!

Before proceeding up the hill just cross the road and note Chad Vara House.

Chad Varah House

As a young curate Chad Vara had been upset and amazed that a young girl whose funeral he had been conducting at St Peters in Eastgate was to be buried in unconsecrated ground because she had committed suicide. The girl had taken her life when she began menstruating and through ignorance she feared she had some awful disease. Vara wanted to do something to overcome such ignorance around sex. He began giving young couples 'talks' and in doing so developed something of an ill informed dubious reputation. He later moved to London and was able to set up a help line for would be suicides and this quickly expanded

according to the need with many call centres attended to by thousands of volunteers. He was ordained in the cathedral and is remembered by a plaque outside the former theological college where he studied now named Chad Vara House. There used to be two medieval churches on this site. These in turn gave way to the Hare and Hounds then the Fighting Cocks which was eventually pulled down to make way for the County Infirmary in 1776. After the new County Hospital was built in 1878 it became a theological college.

Roman South Gate

Further up the hill on the left notice the stone work set into the wall.

These stone blocks are the remains of a Roman gateway. It would have been a large and grand structure with a wide arch and two side arches. Note too the old tea sign.

Widow Cullen's Well

This 16th century building still retains much of its original structure. The well can still be seen under strong glass floor. The story goes that in the 17th century Widow Cullen's yard had the only well in the street so she would have been very popular.

The flags flying in this picture (*above*) are for Lincolnshire day, the 1st October, celebrating the anniversary of the Lincolnshire Rising.

Brown's pie shop

This dates back to the 15th century and is reputedly haunted by a young boy of around eight years old who tormented the chef over many years. Apparently the chef often felt he was being watched and named him Humphrey and used to say hello to him every day to placate him.

Castle Square

This open space is often used for food and craft markets and in December is the hub of the City's famous Christmas Market. It is a good spot to sit and watch the world go by and listen to the buskers.

St Mary Magdalene

This fine old church used to be called Chequer church and its original incarnation stood where the cathedral nave now is but it was swept away by Bishop Regimus to make way for the cathedral. It has a memorial window to E Mansel Sympson a Lincoln born and bred historian. The window depicts St Thomas holding a builders square and St John (*below*).

Mansel Sympson was one time sheriff of the city, a JP, consultant at the County Hospital, governor of the girls high school and much more until his death in 1922. He was also a lieutenant colonel of the RAMC and it was to him the city turned to read the riot act in the 1911 riots. Perhaps the finest aspect of the church are the magnificent carvings on the font (*below*).

Tourist Information Office

This is Leigh-Pemberton House which was built around 1543 and looks the classic Tudor timber framed building. It has in its time been a merchants house, the 'Iron Mongers Arms' and up until 1979 a bank, but now serves appropriately as the Tourist Information Centre (*above*). Robert Leigh Pemberton was the governor of the Bank of England who gave the property to the city.

Note this figure in the corner (*left*).

Judges lodgings

These were built in 1809 to house the judges who came to try cases at the Crown Court in the castle, a function they still retain at times when they are not being used for weddings.

Castle Hill Club

Famous for being the favourite haunt of many an executioner including William Marwood who perfected the long drop method of hanging! It was once the Black Boy inn and it is said that a hostelry has been on this site since 1642 and most probably before that. Isambard Kingdom Brunel stayed here too whilst surveying the Fossdyke Canal. It is home to a replica of the 'Leather Jacket' a leather jug holding 22 pints which was used to quench the thirst of the cathedral bellringers when they had come off duty! When the last pub closed in 1923 the regulars bought it and re-opened it as a member owned club. There are said to be several resident ghosts including the 'bottom pincher'! And the ghost of William Marwood has been reputedly seen peering at the castle out of the window of the room he used to stay in.

LINCOLN CASTLE TO MINSTER YARD

William the Conqueror ordered the building of the Castle shortly after his victory in the battle of Hastings. Whilst he had beaten Harold he still didn't have the support of the local people and so felt it best to build castles to defend his winnings. Lincoln's castle is in a very commanding position overlooking the town, Brayford and wider Witham and Trent basins. In order to site the castle here it is thought he cleared around 160 houses from the top of the hill much to the displeasure of the locals who may have been made to pull down their own houses according to Abel and Chambers (1939). Later bishop Regimus was to choose high ground too for the site of the cathedral and so they were built almost side by side with the clearing of even more locals from their dwellings.

Eastern gate

The Eastern gate is superb in the setting in Castle Square. It used to have a ditch and drawbridge in the 14th century and two towers were built at the end of the drawbridge and enclosed to make a barbican.

If you got through the first gate you were virtually trapped and would fall prey to those firing down on you. These outer towers are now gone but a circle of cobbles near the cannons mark the spot where they once stood.

The castle is noted for having two mounds or 'mottes' as they were called. There is only one other in England at Lewes.

Entrance

Note the fine Oriel window (*right*) which was brought here in 1849 from John of Gaunts palace which used to stand to the south along the high street opposite St Mary's Guildhall. And see if you can find this strange fellow! (*below*)

The walls

Perhaps the most impressive part of the castle is its wall walk where you can make a complete circuit. Built in the early 12th century they give you fine views of the city and surrounding countryside.

Above the barbican you get this fine (*right*) view across Castle square to the cathedral and it is easy to imagine archers firing down on attackers from these battlements as in the battle of Lincoln 1217 when French forces laid siege having taken the city.

Looking back into the castle you have a fine view of the assize courts.

It is also easy to imagine the lawns being used for jousting and archery tournaments and on several occasions each year such an event is spectacularly recreated.

Going anticlockwise you will meet the castles towers beginning with Cobb Hall but look back to catch the fine view of the barbican and observatory tower (*left*).

Cobb Hall

This tower built in the 13th century houses the dungeon. The two stories are vaulted and each held prisoners as you can tell from the iron rings to which they were chained.

They were dismal windowless places with the iron grill the only means of air and escape. Look for the picture of a stag hunt carved into the wall by a prisoner called Thomas Goddard amongst other ancient graffiti.

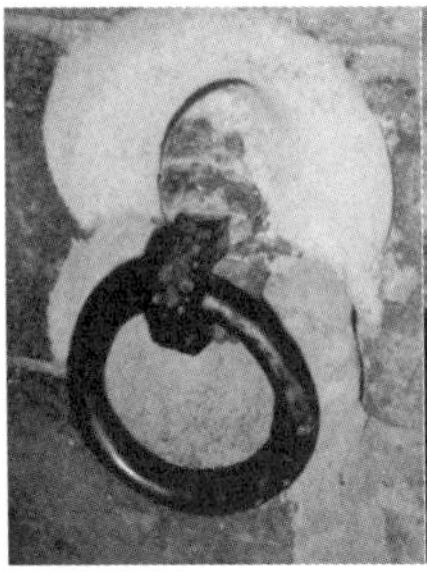

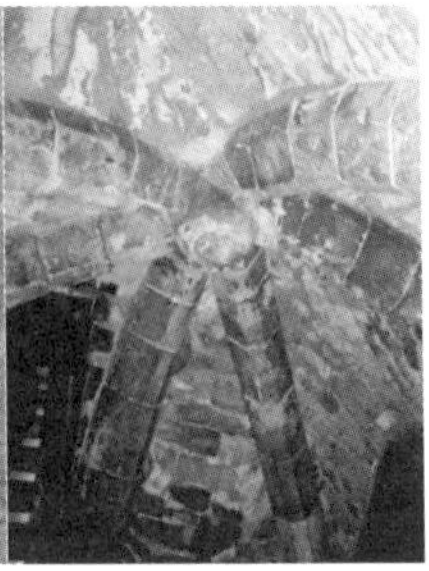

Public executions were held here and from 1817 to 1859 the county gallows stood on Cobb Hall's roof. Look at the view from the top and what you see is the last sight of the world for the condemned man. Hangings back then were a public spectacle with many coming to see villains meet their grisly ends. The last public execution was a double hanging of two young men who after too much to drink murdered an old man for his money. They were so drunk they botched it and were easily apprehended.

Look across to the Georgian prison (*following page, top left*), and as you walk on note the water tower with its city shield (*top right*).

Further around there are fine views along burton road to the north where you will be able to pick out the rear of the 'Strugglers' pub, the sails of Ellis's mill and Trent View flats. This is the view along the limestone 'cliff' which runs north to the Humber and overlooks the Trent basin.

You now cross the West Gate which was built practically next to the old Roman West Gate in what is now the backyard of the Strugglers Inn and it gave access directly to what was then countryside. Now we can see the Lawns complex which used to be Lincolns asylum (*below*).

Beyond this is the West Common and site of the battle of Lincoln 1140.

The Battle of Lincoln

Looking west beyond the Lawns is this likely site of the battle of Lincoln. The 1140 war between King Stephen (William the Conquerors grandson) and Matilda his cousin was a strange and complicated family affair of divided loyalties. Matilda's forces landed in England in 1140 and seized the city and castle briefly but Stephen later recovered them. Then in 1141 the castle changed hands again in the 'Battle of Lincoln' which was fought on the hillside about where the West Common is now. King Stephen was captured and the local citizens who had favoured Stephen were put to the sword and ousted. Matilda had Stephen imprisoned at Bristol and meanwhile attempted to have herself crowned queen but the London people opposed her ... eventually Stephen regained power and the castle returned to his hands in 1146.

At the south west corner you will notice this house which was once owned by the artist Peter de Wint who fell in love with the local landscape (*right*).

On the castle walls lookout for the mosaics of lichens.

Lucy Tower

This keep is thought to be the original Norman Motte (raised earthwork) built in 1110 by Countess Lucy Taillebois, the wife of the then Sherriff of Lincoln Ranulph de Meschines. She was left in charge when he was away checking his various estates and she had it built to give extra protection whilst he was away. It has 15 sides and it never had a roof but would have had lean-to buildings around the inner walls. In the 19th century the bodies of executed convicts were buried here and you can still see two rows of prisoners graves. Tragically there are also two graves of children who were born and died in the prison.

The head stones record the criminals initials and dates of execution.The last recorded execution was that of a William Clarke (alias slenderman!) who was hung in 1877 for shooting a gamekeeper (*above left*).

Note too the grave of Mary Milner (*above middle*) who poisoned her sister in law but stole the hangman's thunder by hanging herself with a neckerchief the night before.

As you move on look back for this fine view of the Lucy Tower and also the prison exercise yards (*above right*).

Observatory tower

This is the other motte of Lincoln's two motte fame!

Somewhere around the beginning of the 19th century the prison governor John Merryweather developed a keen interest in astronomy and added a circular flag turret to this tower near the eastern gate. This was where he kept his star gazing paraphernalia so it is now known as the observatory tower. The views from the top across the city are excellent so see what you can spot. And take a look at this chap on the way back down.

Magna Carta

Housed in a vault by the Georgian Prison the castle has a special exhibition housing an original copy of the Magna Carta on loan from the

An old postcard with a ghostly moonlight observatory tower

cathedral. Only four survive one is at Salisbury Cathedral and two at the British Museum. It dates from the Middle Ages and declares civil rights and democracy. It is enshrined in English Common Law and greatly influences many other charters such as the US Bill of Rights. It basically limited the otherwise excessive royal powers and passed on rights and justice to 'all free men'!

The Victorian prison

The prison was built in 1787, as a replacement for earlier buildings and the Cobb Hall dungeons which were in an appalling state, and was used as a gaol until 1878. It is a grim forbidding place and was ill ventilated with few opening windows so that when it was full the stench was said to be unbearable.

Most inmates here was kept in solitary confinement but when the need arose hammocks were slung across the cells. Lincoln was largely a holding prison and when cholera broke out in London's Millbank prison a backlog grew causing overcrowding.

The exercise yards were small and divided and the inner radiating walls would have been tall to prevent prisoners mixing.

The Prison chapel is a unique experience and was described as an evil place by Marsden (1977). It is a rare Victorian survival. It is designed as a semi-circular theatre like auditorium with ascending rows of individual stalls. These have tall hinged sides as high as a man which kept the prisoners isolated from each other but in full view of the gaolers.

The seats slope down so that you could not sit comfortably and had to half stand! The only thing the prisoners could see was the chaplain preaching at them. It was a clever arrangement so lock yourself in and see how claustrophobic it is! Then stand in the pulpit and try to imagine the miserable prospect of unfortunate faces some hardened maybe and some scared and repentant. The front seats were reserved for female prisoners and the rear stalls for those condemned to death. 'Exceedingly gruesome' according to Morton 1929.

In 1705 Samuel the father of John Wesley was imprisoned here in long lost earlier buildings having been arrested for debt. He'd made enemies of some of his parishioners and they helped see to it that he was hounded and ruined. Imprisonment for debt was a common practice at the time and debtors prisons were often separate from others and the regime usually somewhat more lenient.

Assize Courts

Lincoln Crown Court is still situated within the castle at the assize courts which were built in 1826 and executions were held outside at the southern end from 1859 until 1877. William Marwood from Horncastle was the public executioner for Britain from 1872 until 1883. He is famous for perfecting the hanging technique called the 'long drop' where the weight of the victim

was correlated to the length of rope. This method broke the villain's neck and so gave a quick and merciful death as opposed to a slow strangulation. He became so famous that his gravestone in Horncastle was slowly eroded away by souvenir hunters and he made it into Madamme Tussauds Waxwork's. He carried out 178 executions in his nine year career.

The Bailey

This is the area within the castle walls and is where jousting would have been held. Wander around and look out for the wildlife to be found in the castle at various times of the year. There will almost inevitably be jackdaws and pigeons and often you will find ivy leaved toadflax in nooks and crannies on the walls. In spring there are good displays of daffodils and primroses too.

George III

In the grounds look for the bust of George III (made in 1810) which used to sit atop Dunstan Pillar on the Lincoln heath and limestone cliff just south of the city.

The pillar was commissioned by one Sir Francis Dashwood who moved in high circles and was at one time Chancellor of the Exchequer. It was originally a beacon to help people navigate across Dunston heath. At around 100 ft high the story goes that it was the result of a bet that a stone pillar that high could not be built on a base so narrow. It obviously could but it was damaged in a storm and the beacon was replaced with a bust of George III to celebrate his Golden Jubilee. This was removed to the castle grounds in World War II as it was judged to be a danger to the Lancaster bombers including the Dam Busters who were operational from Lincolnshire's many nearby air bases. Note the impressive

St George and the Dragon he is wearing too (*right*)!

Check out the metallic castle map (*above*), and note too the Norman herring bone patterns in the walls stonework.

Eleanor Cross

Edward 1 had these memorials to his wife made at every nightly resting place of Eleanor of Castile's body on its journey to London to be buried. This stump is the lower half of a statue showing her gown. But it is still a grade II listed stump! Her viscera were interred at the cathedral and she was embalmed at the Gilbertine priory of St Catherine, near the south common where this cross originally stood. You can visit the Priory Heritage Centre for a more detailed insight into this important aspect of Lincoln's history. (www.priorylincoln.co.uk)

Carved tree stump

Look closely at the carved tree stump where you will find a range of people who lived at the castle at one time such as William the Conqueror.

In 1066 Halley's comet was seen in England prior to the battle of Hastings. William when seeing it took it as an omen that his invasion plans would succeed.

See if you can spot the duck too!

Exit the Castle by the West gate and cross the road into the Lawns complex.

The Lawns

Originally known as the 'Lincoln Asylum' this was built in 1819 as a private hospital for the treatment of the insane. It was the county's first asylum and

the first Doctor in charge was one E D Charlesworth. He was famous for pioneering systems of 'non restraint' and more humane methods of treatment than were the norm at the time. In particular he was against the use of solitary confinement and straight-jackets. Charlesworth replaced mechanical restraint with 'attention' and 'useful occupation'. Simply doing away with some locks meant that the 'attendants' had to pay their charges some attention! Clients were also put to work in book keeping, the laundry, gardening and in the kitchens. Entertainment was also regarded as therapy with a monthly ball and visits to fairs, concerts, the Cathedral and even to the seaside and the races! In her pamphlet 'One hundred and fifty years at the Lawn' Beatrice Louise Melton tells us how the patients would dine with the medical super-intendant and that some gentleman were allowed into the ladies quarters for cards and music. She tells us that ... 'nothing is so detrimental to the manners and savoir-faire as isolation'. At its height it housed 145 patients and did not close until the 1980s. One of the hospitals supporters and instigators was Dr Francis Willis who treated King George III's malady, a subject well told in the film *The Madness of King George*. By 1841 The Lawns had 101 patients mostly local paupers and by 1852 it had 145. That year a new hospital 'St Johns' was built in Bracebridge and The Lawns became the preserve of 'paying patients'.

In the grounds the Charlotte House hotel is named after Charlotte Benner the first Lawns matron from 1820 to 1833 and it used to be the nurses quarters from 1938. The rules dictated that the matron must be Church of England, no older than 40, unmarried and with no children. In 1820 her salary was around £25 a year.

Look for the statue of Charlesworth in the south east corner of the grounds.

From here peer through the railings at 'Hilton House' house opposite. This was built by the Lincoln artist William Hilton and both he and Peter De Wint lived here. Also in the grounds you will find the Joseph Banks Conservatory. The botanist Banks was the son of a Lincolnshire Landowner and this tropical greenhouse displays some of the plants discovered by him when he sailed in the *Endeavour* with Captain Cook on his voyage to discover Australia. On leaving the Lawns pop into the Victoria pub for a well earned rest and to sample the fare of the Lincolnshire brewery of Batemans.

Union Road and Occupation Lane ... a bit of history you can't see!

Coming out of the lawns onto Union Road reminds us that this area was close to the site of Lincolns Poor Law Union workhouse. Now head down Burton road and note too 'Occupation Lane'. This used to lead down to the 'House of Industry'.

Was this the workhouse main drive perhaps?

This workhouse existed from around 1740 but now little trace of it remains. It was basically for paupers and discipline was reputedly severe. Yeates-Langley (2009) sets the scene telling us that women were employed as 'nurses' to wash and comb the children and that many illegitimate children were born within its walls. Other women were made to spin hemp and the men break stones or work in the garden. Children were also sent out to work, boys reputedly as chimney sweeps and the girls into domestic service, but there was also a school on the premises. The residents all wore the house uniform and the men and boys wooden clogs. Many died in the workhouse and were buried at St Pauls in the Bail, the outline of which can be seen next to Lloyds bank in Bailgate. This workhouse was demolished in 1839 and replaced by the new Lincoln Union Workhouse. This housed 269 of the poor, the old or the ill, alongside unmarried mothers and their illegitimate offspring. The mentally ill and disabled were also admitted but at the time unemployment and having no means of support was a large factor for men being admitted. Yeates-Langley speaks of the diet being even more meagre than that of the preceding house of industry where the luxury of a beer was occasionally had. Again a uniform had to be worn, basically shapeless but the clogs had been replaced by hobnail boots. Up at 6am in summer to work from 8am until 6pm at stone breaking, sack making, laundry or gardening with an hour for a lunch of bread, broth and a sliver of meat, some potatoes and suet dumplings. In such austerity families were not allowed to meet together and women were allowed around one hour a week to see their children. From 1848 there was also a Penitent Females Home backing onto Carline Road which was formerly Asylum Road as it ran past The Lawns. It housed 25 abandoned women 'to reclaim them to the habits of industry and virtue' and employed them in pursuits such as laundry and needlework to train them for domestic service. Continue down Burton Road until you come upon the Museum of Lincolnshire Life.

Museum of Lincolnshire Life to Newport Arch

This museum perfectly describes itself as a 'cornucopia of yesteryear'! It is housed in an old army barracks built in 1857 for the Royal North Lincoln Militia.

They were part time volunteers whose main role was home defence. From 1901 it was home to the Lincolnshire Yeomanry and was in use by the military until 1969. The 1881 census shows some of the barracks were used as an overspill for the nearby workhouse whilst it was being enlarged. In shape it is a large red brick quadrangle and on the north side were quarters for six officers and their families, the south side was the drill hall.

The museum has an intriguing collection of items relating to social history with many rooms and shops recreated as they would have been years ago.

The museum also celebrates the fact that Lincoln is the birth place of the tank. This was developed by the firm of Fosters and its managing director, Sir William Tritton, is credited with its invention.

The battlefields of Flanders were like soggy ploughed fields so it is no surprise that the solution for transport across them should come from engineering firms used to making agricultural machinery. The tank soon became essential for crossing the trenches in World War I.

There is much to enjoy here so see if you can find these items on display ...

The window was designed by Edward Burne Jones for William Morris and Co as part of a war memorial for St Marks church which used to stand in the High Street but was demolished in 1971.

Leaving the museum turn right and right again down Long Leys Road and take the first right down Mill Road.

Ellis' Mill

Dating from around 1798 this is the only survivor of a long line of nine windmills from medieval times which used to stand along this limestone ridge. In fact Mill Road used to be called Mills Road! The demise of the mills is largely down to the rise of steam powered mills in the latter half of the 19th century. This black painted red brick tower mill bears the name of the Ellis family who owned it from 1894 to 1973. It was threatened with demolition but listed and in 1977 the Lincoln Civic Trust began its restoration. It is now a conglomeration of parts from other local but destitute mills. It had ceased operating in 1916 but ground flour again in 1981.

Retrace your steps back towards the castle and walk down Westgate.

The Strugglers

A strong contender for best pub in Lincoln and certainly one which preserves a traditional pub ambience with real beer, locals and a fantastic 'landlady'. It's almost like walking back into the Museum of Lincolnshire Life and well deserves all the awards it wins. This corner of Westgate was known as Hangmans Ditch and is where hangings took place until 1815. The pub name refers to the 'reluctance' of the condemned as they were dragged towards the scaffold. When people were hung it would usually take them some time to die and they would invariably thrash and struggle as they slowly choked and so their friends would pull on their legs to hasten their end. Such 'friends' were called 'hangers on'. In those days prisoners were often hung in batches and the occasions were public spectacles with large crowds often into the thousands coming to watch. The pub is said to be haunted by a lurcher which belonged to a chap called William Clark who was hung here in 1877.

Water Tower

This was completed in 1911 after a tragic outbreak of typhoid in 1904/5. 113 people died in the epidemic which was caused by contaminated water from the city's reservoir in Hartsholme. The Town Corporation and Water Board had pipes laid from a new water supply in Elkesley, Nottinghamshire 22 miles away and Lincoln became one of the first places to use chlorine to disinfect the water supply. The tower reputedly holds 330,000 gallons enough to supply uphill Lincoln for a day!

The architect Sir Reginald Bloomfield is said to have designed it to look like a castle keep and blend in with the rest of the city's Medieval heritage. It is an imposing building at 110 ft high but get close up and look upwards to really appreciate this.

There is some nice decoration notably the shield and all the fleur-de-lys in the upper sections. These are the symbol of The Virgin Mary, Patron Saint of Lincoln.

Walking up Chapel Lane lookout for these more modern insignia.

Newport Arch

This North gateway of the Roman city spanning Ermine Street is reputed to be the best surviving Roman gateway in Britain. These gateways were status symbols but what we see today is but a small fraction of the original. It would have been significantly taller because the ground level has risen considerably by about 8 feet. It would also have been a tunnel with smaller tunnels either side. Outside these would have been large defensive bastions to protect the walls and the remains of one can be seen just through the arch. Soldiers would patrol the top and man the gatehouse. The arch we see today is just the south face end of the gatehouse tunnel.

Morton (1929) suggests that the smaller arch for foot passengers was called the 'needles eye' after the biblical parable. It is so named after a gate in Jerusalem through which a camel could only pass with its baggage removed and upon its knees! So in Jerusalem after the main city gates had closed the rich merchants had to leave their camels laden with goods outside and enter the city through the eye of the needle.

The arch is also famed for being the only Roman gateway in the UK with traffic still going through it. Inevitably damaged and partially demolished by lorries and buses over the years, what we see today has been often repaired. Much traffic still passes through it but cast your mind back to Roman times and imagine soldiers on horseback, chariots and marching legions passing under the arch. Abel and Chambers (1939) tell us that the Roman walls connecting these gateways and surrounding the city would have been some 18 feet high.

Newport

When locals were cleared from their homes for the building of the cathedral some of them settled in a new suburb just north of the arch. This grew and had its own market and church dedicated to St Nicholas (the patron saint of merchants). Most of the new settlers were traders who bought their goods to sell at the gates of the old city, thus a new market or new port.

Many such traders were wool and cloth merchants. And the most important craft guilds, and the first in Lincoln, were the weavers and dyers guilds. Lincoln was especially well known for its red cloth and the Lincoln Green that was supposed to have been worn by Robin Hood and his merry men. Legend also has it that Robin Hood clad himself in scarlet on special occasions. This red cloth was more expensive as its dye was derived from a Mediterranean beetle. Because of this it was often stolen. Much of this contraband was still damp when it was stolen as it was hung out drying. Capturing the thieves was somewhat easy as many were ‘caught red handed’ or ‘taken with red hand’! Hence the expression. A Scottish version has it that the expression means to be caught in the act.

Bailgate

This area is so named as the area was the castle’s Outer Bailey. As the city itself grew so too did conflict with the Constable of the castle who ruled both over his troops and those who lived in the Outer Bailey of the castle or the ‘Bail’. The city authorities set up boundary stones on the side of road leading through the gateways of the Roman city and by the side of the moat marking the limits of the Bail or the area governed by the castle Constable. They can be seen by Eastgate and on Steep Hill. On your way towards the cathedral keep an eye out for this above a low doorway.

Inside the north gate (Newport arch) there would have been a forum or market square and basilica or town hall. A few yards further on note the round cobbles set into the pavement which mark the position of columns of a Roman colonnade and may have been part of just such a basilica or forum.

Opposite are the County Assembly Rooms, an 18th century building used for events and celebrations.

Lincoln's oldest church

Crossing back over Westgate you encounter the remains the church of St Paul in the Bail next to Lloyds Bank. Now a quiet corner, it was Lincoln's oldest church (and one of Britain's) being mentioned by Bede as being built by Paulinus in the 7th century around AD 629. When the last church was demolished in 1971, excavations revealed a Roman well. Prior to that the well is thought to have determined the location for the church, which is unusual.

There have been five incarnations of the church on this site in all. Now just the footprint of the church, as it was in 1786, is preserved along with some of the original gravestones. The bank next door is another lost pub as it used to be the Scarborough and the Lion and Snake opposite used to be called The Ram. Step into the road carefully here and you will see the row of roman columns continuing, indicating the size of the development.

The White Hart

This is reputedly one of the most haunted buildings in Lincoln and its modern upmarket persona belies the fact that it was once known as a haunt of thieves and other undesirables. One such was a highwayman who tried to rob a coach but the coachman thrust a burning torch into his face

delivering him an agonising death before carrying on to the White Hart. The disfigured highwayman now roams the coach yard and corridors looking for his assailant seeking to extract revenge for his hideous fate. Those who have seen him testify that his eyes still glare from his disfigured face. Many other ghost stories centre upon the hotel and at nights it is said that many have heard Roman soldiers marching by or a coach and horses entering the yard!

The building is reputed to date originally from around 1387 in Richard II's reign and his emblem is a white hart. It is obviously much restored and what we see today dates from 1710 when it was a typical coaching inn. Where the White Hart garage is used to be the Swan Inn until the late 18th century. The ice cream parlour next door was built around 1720 but has roots back to medieval times in its vaulted cellar.

Watsons the chemist

This is one of the longest running businesses in Lincoln. Frederick Percy Watson, born Lincoln 1865, bought the business in the 1890s and it still bears his name long after his death. This was originally the site of yet another pub, the 13th century Antelope Inn, until around 1840.

Now head down Eastgate opposite Watsons.

The Black Horse Chambers and the Dean's wife!

Before you walk up here be mindful that there used to be an arched gate house between White Hart and Post Office. Halfway down look out for what is now Cathedral View guest house. This is another of Lincoln's lost pubs, dating back to the 13th century the building became the Black Horse Chambers in the 17th century.

This too is said to be haunted ... by a grey lady and some chap called Julian! Cross the road and head away from the Bail and you will see a curious gargoyle's head sticking out of the stone wall and seemingly looking directly at the Black Horse.

In the pubs early days it was much used by the cathedral clergy, allegedly often drinking to excess, and legend has it that the Bishop of Lincoln had it put there to remind them of their 'other' calling and that he and God were keeping an eye on their nocturnal drinking habits. Others call her the Dean's wife saying that she is checking that the Dean turns down Minster Yard to the cathedral and not across the road to the pub. Another story tells of a pub regular whose wife always worried about him and one night when he hadn't returned she leant out of the sash window to look out for him when it came down upon her and broke her neck. He was said to have been heartbroken (of course!) and had her head carved and placed in the wall as a memorial. A more likely view is that this is simply a piece of one of the many cathedral statues Cromwell's men destroyed which has since been amusingly placed in the wall. Now turn down Minster Yard to the Exchequer Gate.

Exchequer Gate

The main entrance to the close was via Exchequergate and all gates were double gates except for Pottergate where the steepness deemed this precaution unnecessary and Greestone where it was also too steep to need it. The gates were all closed at night to keep undesirables out.

The church was a huge landowner and Exchequergate was where tenants came to pay their rent. The three-storey, three-arched gate has a large central arch with a postern gate on either side. Apparently a public house was kept in the apartment to the north of the southern postern called the 'Great Tom Inn' after the cathedral bell. Look for the bricked up openings in the walls of the passages where relics, beads and rosaries and the like would have been sold.

It would originally have been a double gateway enclosing the courtyard in between but only the inner one is left ... if you look at the wall of St Mary Magdalene's you can see two blank windows testifying to the existence of the outer one as does a 1795 painting of it by J M W Turner.

Hooks for the hinges of the doors can still be seen in the arches (*below left*) but notice especially the vaulting and bosses (*middle left*). One in the northern arch has a representation of the crucifixion on it (*middle right*). And another in the South arch has either a castle or the close with gate and towers depicted (*right*) ... which do you think?

And maybe this is a pilgrim!

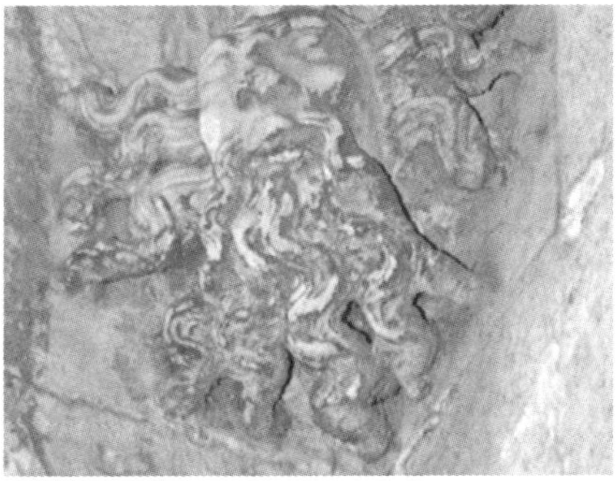

Make sure you find the 'sunny beard'!

And on the outside is this a monkey?

And who is this lady?

Look for this sombre chap.

Is this another Lincoln Imp turned to stone … I think so.

What dignitary or saint used to stand proud here?

Minster Yard

The area around the cathedral is known as Minster Yard. Medieval Lincoln was split into three areas ... City, Castle Bail and Cathedral Close and each was independently governed. The Close was the area around the cathedral where priests and cathedral officials and their servants lived. The dean and chapter held a weekly court for disputes within the close and they were free from interference from the castle and city. They had their own market and kept the market tolls, contributing nothing to the city taxes thus annoying the city governors and mayor.

In the 12th century this was a very wealthy area and was often frequented by thieves, murderers and robbers or according to the 1899 Boots cash chemists *Guide to Lincoln* 'cut-purses and other evil doers'! The law of the city did not apply in the cathedral close and those charged with crime in the city would flee to the sanctuary of the close to avoid arrest. Because of this the dean and chapter were granted licences to enclose it and in 1285 a twelve foot wall was built with locked gates to be closed at dusk. In 1318 a licence was granted to strengthen it and embattle it with turrets and raise it further.

LINCOLN CATHEDRAL EXTERIOR

The cathedrals central tower stands 271 feet high on Lincoln's limestone edge; it is a magnificent site dominating the skyline as you approach Lincoln from the South. However it's not until you get close that you begin to understand just how magnificent it is. Yates and Thorold (1965) called the view of the cathedral from downhill 'one of the great sights of Europe'. John Ruskin was also smitten and of the opinion that Lincoln cathedral was worth two of any others and that it was the most precious piece of architecture in the British Isles. It is easy to fall in with this view and be seduced by its majesty, but one needs to remember the blood, sweat, tears and skill that went into building it. The cathedral has undergone several tragedies notably an earth quake and a fire only to be rebuilt and subsequently robbed of much of its finery and treasure by Henry VIII and then its brasses torn up and statues, tombs and stained glass smashed in the civil war by the Royalists ... twice.

According to Kendrick (1898) the contemporary diarist 'John Evelyn', recorded in 1654 that the soldiers 'went in with axes and hammers, and shut themselves in, till they had rent and torn off some barge loads of metal, not even sparing the monuments of the dead; so hellish an avarice possessed them'. Even given this damage the Cathedral is still a wonder and it is hard to imagine what it might have been like had it not been so thoroughly ransacked and its treasures floated down the Witham to fund the extravagances of Henry VIII and others.

You will see literally hundreds of empty pedestals like this one (*far left*) as you walk around tempting the thought of what must have been when all the missing statues were still in place and before Cromwell and the like left their mark. One of the biggest delights of the cathedral however remains the skill and quirky humour of the stonemasons and woodcarvers. Any gargoyle is an obvious testament to this but you will discover an embarrassment of weird delights if you look that bit deeper (*left*).

As you explore the cathedral also remind yourself that it was built pre health and safety and pre-JCB with wooden scaffolding, ropes and pulleys, plumb lines and dodgy wooden platforms high above.

It was begun by the Normans in 1072 and suffered a fire in 1141 and the earthquake on 15th April, 1185 destroyed most of the Norman church and according to Srawley (1947) 'the metropolitan church of Lincoln was rent asunder from top to bottom'. What remains of the Norman church can still be seen in the arched doorways of the West Front. St Hugh of Avalon was appointed Bishop by Henry II in 1186 and began the rebuilding in 1192. The cathedral was not finished until around 1280 with additions and repairs being made every now and again until the late 17th century. The majority of the stone used was local Oolitic limestone. Get up close to some of the smooth pillars by the doors and see if you can spot any fossils.

Most visitors to Cathedrals make a beeline for the West Front in all its magnificence and never think to explore more of the outside but here one will find much decoration, ornament and the wit of the stonemason, so take a stroll around the exterior before you sample the riches inside.

Top tip

Take a pair of binoculars to inspect the outside so that you can really appreciate the gargoyles and details above you. They are also useful for spotting the nesting peregrine falcons in the summer.

West Front

William the Conqueror appointed Lincoln's first Bishop, Regimus who came from Normandy. Regimus began to build the cathedral around 1074 but died four days before it was due to be consecrated in 1092. The central doorway and the two deep recesses either side show the extent of this first building. According to the precentor Venebles, quoted in the 1899 Boots cash chemists *Guide to Lincoln*, it was characterised by a 'stern, almost savage plainness'. Within these thick walls are passages and chambers accessible from inside only. The three doorways are in elaborate contrast to the Norman wall and are the work of Bishop Alexander. The central doorway has four columns on either side carved with grotesques and elaborate mouldings which are carried around the arch. Study it closely and see if you can find the features shown in the photographs on the following two pages ...

The Frieze

After the fire in 1141 Bishop Alexander elaborated the west front and added the friezes of Old and New Testament incidents. They also contained illustrations of the cardinal sins such as greed lust and sodomy. They have been mixed up over the years with rebuildings and repairs so are in no particular order. Some are considered to be of Saxon origin or even earlier from the church of St Mary Magdalene which previously stood on this spot. It is thought that they would have been painted and even more striking.

left to right: *An archer aiming his arrow at a bottom above?*
Adam and Eve eating apples (or sucking their thumbs!);
Some sort of exchange occurring here! Postman maybe or is it a bribe!

above: *Note too these bizarre and elaborate mouldings, and these pillar patterns.*

below: *Can you spot these?*

And these ornate 11th century capitals on the doorway

Notice the classical Norman arches

There seems to be an Egyptian theme here too!

and above them the statues of eleven kings from William the Conqueror to Edward III. Originally these would have been coloured, gilt and even more impressive.

The friezes are being restored but see if you can pick out ...

Six saints in conference

Christ the 'custodian' of all faithful souls sitting on a throne holding a sheet with three souls on it. The four apostles are in the corners

Christ releasing souls from the jaws of hell and standing triumphant on the prostrate devil

Dives feasting with no time for Lazarus

The death of Lazarus with Dives and his companions underneath in hell?

Other panels are being repaired but include ... Adam and Eve expelled from paradise, two men tilling the soil probably meant to signify the condemnation of man to toil and labour, the building of the ark with Noah clutching a hammer and a son with an axe, the ark in the background and Daniel in a particularly scary lions' den! Watch out too for the panels depicting punishment for adultery and sexual sins.

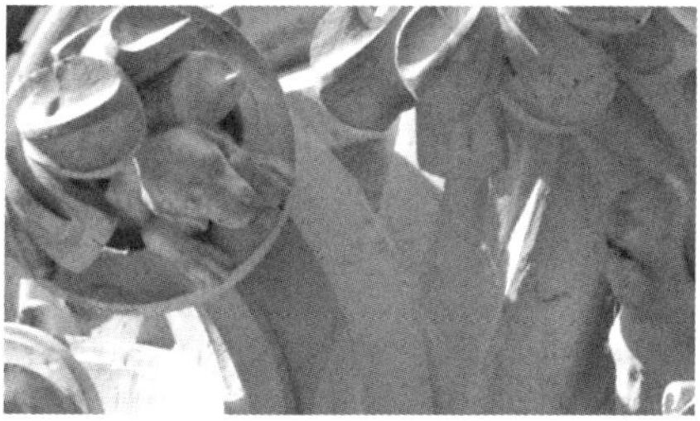

By the left hand door look for the modern sculpture commemorating Lincolnshire's tradition of fox hunting, look for the horse and hounds. And see if you can spot where the fox is hiding (*above*).

Note the quality of the old wooden doors too (*right*).

The West Front is flanked with octagonal stair turrets with small pyramidal roofs. The south one is Bishop St Hugh of Avalon with staff and mitre.

The other is Gurth the Swineherd of Stow blowing his horn (*right*). He is said to have gifted the cathedral builders a peck of silver pennies (all his savings) thus securing his statue a prominent position.

South side exterior

At the head of the tall central lancet is a grotesque said to be the devil looking over Lincoln. Though local legend has it that it can't be as he is still inside afraid to come out for fear of being blown away. Curious as it is this south western corner of the cathedral is by far the windiest spot in Lincoln. A quirk of the surrounding architecture maybe or something more sinister perhaps! Note too the two pilgrims looking up at him.

There are many gargoyles, statues and grotesques along these walls and projecting from above you so use your binoculars to inspect them.

Galilee porch

This was fashioned in 1230 as a state entrance for the bishop whose palace is just over the cobbles. It is designed in the form of a cross and the doorway is richly carved with dog teeth and foliage (*above*). Apparently there are 5,355 dog teeth on the porch!

Note two 12th or 13th century stone coffin covers on the floor and the pillar shafts with human headed beasts around the foot (*right*)!

Around the corner from this porch you will find a recess which most people ignore but which holds these gems. A greedy banker, perhaps a reminder of modern times! Note the gold coin in his mouth.

And this, maybe a reminder of what becomes of those who succumb to greed!

Watch out for those claws! But look up to find further delights from old and modern stonemasons alike. Check out the puzzled monkey stonemason!

And the person with the bucket and bunch of keys, and who's this chap at the top of the drain pipe ... and what's he doing there?

Central Tower

It is 271 feet to the top of the pinnacle but the wooden spire which once topped it was said to reach to 525 feet. All three towers originally had spires and the central tower was once the tallest structure in Europe. The central spire was blown down in a tempest in 1548. The original central tower fell down around 1237 at the time of Bishop Grosseteste. At the four corners are octagonal turrets with pinnacles. Kendrick (1898) cites a certain Sir Charles Anderson who cites a certain 'Walcott' as saying that the tower is 'so full of state and dignity, and majestic grandeur, that no church in England, or on the continent, can be cited in the same description'. Apparently the perfect symmetry and strength is due to its being 'gathered in' about 2½ inches 25 feet below the parapet ... 'which shews upon what trifles, as they might be called, beauty and proportion depend'!

In the summer look for nesting peregrines and the somewhat blasé pigeons! These feral pigeons are descended from wild rock doves who nest on seas cliffs. Here they find the cathedral and castle walls a suitable cliff substitute.

Sundial

This two faced dial allows you to tell the time as the sun moves around the cathedral. This picture was taken in mid winter at noon.

The Judgement Porch

This beautiful piece of sculpture depicting the day of judgement was, like the Galilee door, made as a state entrance for the Bishop giving access into the Angel Choir. Many suggest that it is one of the finest doorways in the country. The central relief is set in a quatrefoil with a central figure of Christ flanked by two angels. This itself is supported by four angels and on one side are the righteous rising from their tombs being borne to heaven by the angels and on the other are the 'others' being dragged down by demons to the 'gaping jaws of hell' (Srawley 1947).

Over the quatrefoil are three carved arches. In the first is a series of canopied kings and queens, in the second a band of richly cut foliage and in the third are figures illustrating the parable of the wise and foolish virgins.

There is also a beautiful Madonna and child (*right*) between the two doors and it is these doors through which pilgims to the shrine of St Hugh would have come and gone.

Near the porch is a buttress with a gargoyle of a devil on a witches back and some consider this to be another imp who when he tried to hitch a lift on the unfortunate hunchback turned

to stone. Another gargoyle appears to show a woman playing the bagpipes! (*previous page*)

The statue on a nearby buttress (*right*) was said to be Queen Margaret of Valois who Edward I married after Queen Eleanor's death. It is a life like statue of a beautiful smiling woman holding the graceful drapery of her gown, considered by Arthur Mee to be 'one of the loveliest pieces of medieval sculpture in the land'.

Edward I and Eleanor have statues on another buttress (*left*). Edward is trampling on a Saracen.

East Front (the back)

As you round the corner note that the path is the route of the old city wall. The hexagonal structure with a pyramidal roof was the cathedral well (*next page*).

Take the time to check out the North side of the Angel choir where a door has a worn shield of arms in front of the capitol which is that of Richard II (*above*).

Chapter House exterior

The walls are strengthened with superb flying buttresses on some of which marks can be seen where houses were once built against them ... sacrilege!

Tennyson Statue

This is a fine tribute to Lincolnshire's greatest Poet. It was designed and sculpted by his friend George Frederick Watts. It is apparently unfinished and Watts died before it was cast in 1903. One of his finest works, it depicts Tennyson contemplating a flower with his Siberian Wolfhound, Karenina, at his side.

On this corner of Eastgate and Priorygate there once stood one of the oldest pubs in Lincoln, the 14th century Dolphin. It was also owned by the dean and chapter but was eventually bought by local entrepreneur Alfred Shuttleworth who lived over the road and he had it demolished because it spoilt his view of the cathedral!

Priory Gate

This arched gateway is an 1816 Victorian replacement for the Medieval one that once stood here. The current gateway has battlements and it would have been guarded as it gives access to the cathedral close.

Pottergate

Along here at number 6 lived the one time Cathedral organist and composer William Byrd.

Byrd, a Londoner, was appointed the master of the choristers and cathedral organist in 1563 when he was just 24 and remained in post until 1572. He was a pupil of the organist and composer Thomas Tallis with whom he went on to work and compose. He became probably the most famous Elizabethan composer and wrote music for practically every medium but it is for his choral, Latin and organ work he is most renowned. He was a firm Roman Catholic which often brought him into conflict with the Elizabethan state but he enjoyed the patronage and protection of Elizabeth I. *Ave Verum Corpus* is a good introduction to his work and is considered by many to be William Byrd's finest piece. He died on 4th July, 1623.

The Chancery

Thought to be Lincoln's oldest brick building it was built around 1316 but the red brick and fine Oriel window were added around the1480s. It was at one time the home of Katherine Swynford, wife of John of Gaunt.

Also along Pottergate is a house once occupied by George Boole the mathematician of Boolean logic fame he opened a school at 3 Pottergate and there is a memorial to him there.

Pottergate Arch

A 14th century traffic island! This gateway protected the Southern entrance to the close and takes its name from the tradition that a Roman pottery stood on the site. Most arches of the Cathedral Close were double arches but the hill up to Pottergate was deemed so steep as to only need one arch. Above the arch was a chamber for the gatekeeper and you can still see the fireplace corbelled out of the north front with its embattled chimney.

Just over the road is the Adam and Eve pub which dates back to around 1701 and has a nice steeply pitched pantile roof.

But cross into the island and look back through the arch to the cathedral towers.

Now head back to the cathedral West Front entrance.

LINCOLN CATHEDRAL INTERIOR

Vestibule

As you step into the vestibule note the doors into the walls which are so thick as to have passages within them (*right*). Indeed Bishop Regimus used to live in the west front which was fortified in Norman times. A roof tour will occasionally let you into the spiral staircases and rooms of the west front. It used to house twenty or so soldiers and as the stairs rise they get narrower so that they could be defended by one soldier with a sword.

Nave

The word Nave comes from the Latin 'Navis' for ship and if you look up at the ribbed vaulting you can see how it resembles the ribs in the keel of an upturned ship. The nave is vast and is supported by huge limestone and Purbeck marble pillars. Just stand here a while and take in the huge sense of space. Look for names painted on the ceiling like Fricabon. These are the names of some of those who contributed to the building.

Walk down the right hand aisle.

Font

The square font is made from black Tournai marble and dates to around the middle of the 12th century. This is a form of limestone which when finished by polishing and waxing gives the appearance of black marble. It is actually a self assembly kit! It was carved in workshops close to the source in Belgium and exported in pieces. They became very fashionable and were almost mass produced and are to be found all over Europe.

Notice the mythical beasts carved on the font which are said to represent the fight between good and evil or original sin which baptism is said to remove.

South Aisle

Continuing down the aisle notice these scenes in the windows (*from top of next page, clockwise from top left*) ...

David and Goliath
The Good Samaritan
Moses and the burning bush
The angel stopping Abraham slaying Isaac
Joshua

JOSHUA
JOSHUA

EBED

When bright sun shines through these windows it creates a magical light display on the pillars.

The cathedral was built in the shape of a cross but became slightly out of kilter when being rebuilt. Walk under the central tower and look back up the nave along the mid rib towards the entrance and see if you can tell.

The round window in the west front you see as you look back down the nave depicts Bishop Regimus holding the cathedral.

The Tower

The central tower collapsed in 1237 shortly after it was built. The story goes that when Bishop Grossteste inspected the building works the dean and chapter resisted, perhaps as they did not want him to inspect their shoddy building work! However he persisted and inside found only bare walls. The bishop berated his canons and the precentor took the

opportunity to preach a sermon against the 'interfering' bishop saying 'such are the deeds of this man that if we were to hold our peace the very walls would cry out' ... this was followed by a rumbling sound as the recently built central tower came crashing down. Maybe this chapter house window depicts the very moment! (*see bottom of previous page*)

It was not rebuilt until 1311 and is often described as the richest tower in England. It rests on four arches supported by massive piers surrounded by shafts of Purbeck marble. Look up under the centre and gaze at the vaulting and bosses and note the off centre trap door for getting the bells up into the tower. There is a walkway under the arches with small bridges across the corners.

Climb the 340 steps to the top from where superb views of the town and countryside can be had and, on a clear day, you can see Boston Stump almost 30 miles way. The tower held the bell Great Tom which weighed about 4½ tons. It had to stop tolling in 1802 as according to the Stamford Mercury it was found to 'injure the tower where he hangs'. The article goes on to describe how the bell was chained so that 'instead of the full mouthful he has been used to send forth, he is enjoined in future merely to wag his tongue'. In 1827 the bell was found to be cracked and it was broken up along with six other bells and sent to London to be recast and finally returned weighing around 5½ tons and at over 6 feet high the mind boggles as to how they got it back up there!

The South transept

Works chantry

Here are three linked chapels.

This was dedicated to St Edward the Martyr to provide prayers for the benefactors of the church and was also called the Founders Chapel. Note the four chantry priests (headless) and inscription around the arch and the seated bishop occupying the spandrel above the entrance arch. Inside look for this contemporary sculpture (*left*).

According to Mansel Sympson (1906) St Hugh himself 'laboured' with his own hands in this chapel and a cripple was miraculously cured after using the hod which Bishop Hugh had used. Note too the 'double vaulting' or arcading which you will see often here. It was said to be a form favoured by Bishop Hugh. Some historians suggest that when the roof vaults were being put in place it was realised that the walls needed to be thicker so they made them wider but didn't want to cover up the lovely arches they had already made so invented this double arcading to overcome the problem.

The second chapel is dedicated to St John the Evangelist and the third to St Thomas. Note the elaborate altar tomb of Sir George Talboys.

Bishops Eye

This 14th century window has beautiful tracery likened to two leaves side by side and the glass whilst just fragments of Early English glass non

the less glows with colour. It is called the Bishops Eye because it looks out over the Bishops Palace. Another story has it that the window looks to the sunny south to invite the Holy Spirit whilst the opposite Deans Eye guards against the devils approach from the north. Note the elaborate framing stonework.

Look at the four lancet windows depicting Christ holding a redeemed soul in his robe, the kiss of Judas, the last supper and Herods banquet with Herodias's daughter 'tumbling' in scarlet stockings before him.

In an adjoining window Christ and St Peter walk on water (*right*).

On the east facing wall note this macabre scene (*below, right*).

Note too the monument to the rather rotund Samuel Fuller (*below*).

The Choir screen

Bishop Grossteste and his stonemasons are responsible for the elaborate decorated style screen and the superb mouldings over the aisle arches. These according to Mansell Sympson are 'beyond praise' and 'as perfect a specimen as it is possible to find'.

Get up close and see if you can find ... The stone mason himself with his chisel and stonemason's cap (*right*).

Then see if you can find this lonely owl (*below*).

Most of the carvings are of grotesques so see if you can find this little creature.

And this 'cheeky' mooning man!

Note the blue, red and gold colours here and in other parts of the screen these are relics of medieval times when much of the cathedral was brightly painted. The gold would have been real gold as it was originally 'gilded' with gold leaf.

Find this carved pillar and its paint remains. The figures atop these pillars are bishops (*right*).

Now see if you can spot this monkey eating an orange,

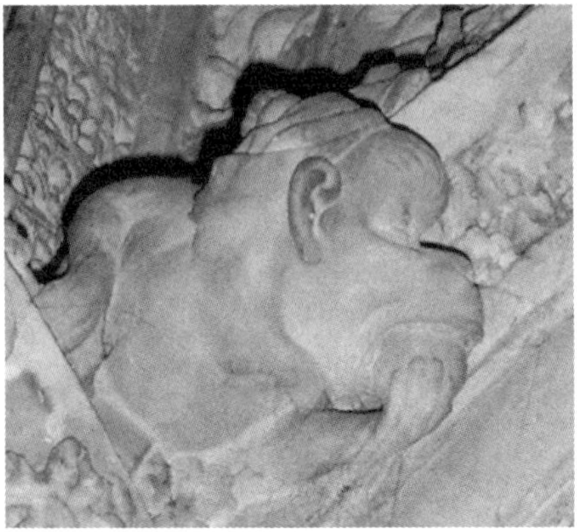

and the Hunchback of Lincoln!

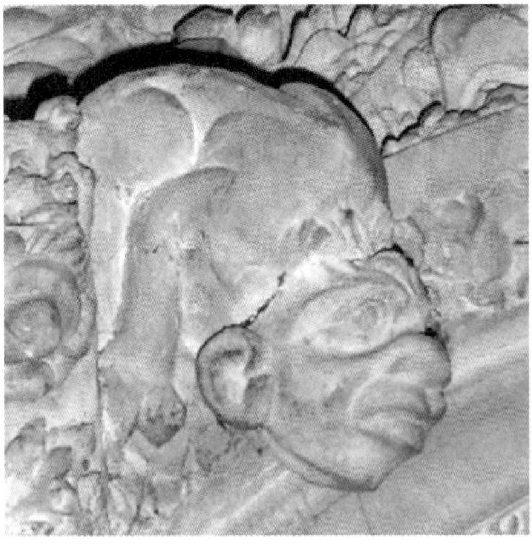

And the lion a medieval symbol of strength.

Organ

The organ case designed by E J Wilson now encloses an organ built by Allen in 1826 and repaired by Willis in 1898. The organist in 1702 was one John Reading who composed *Adeste Fidelis … O Come all ye Faithful.*

The South choir aisle doorway

The doorway just right of the choir screen is slightly earlier than the screen being Early English and is remarkable in its intricacy. Check out two small owls looking from a capital which are looking at the dragons being slayed opposite.

Note this and other dragons looking like they are trying to eat the pillars! (*above middle*) On the opposite side the carving represents dragons stealing grapes whilst the men try to stop them with swords (*above*). Above the door to the south choir aisle notice the very intricate hollow 'openwork' foliage arch which give yet more testament to the immense skill of these craftsmen (*right*).

South Choir Aisle

Notice the carved foliage capitals and the double arcading here (*right*).

And find the one with acorns (*above*).

Note here the double arcade of richly moulded trefoil headed arches in front and plain arches behind. The external moulding being dogtooth and between each trefoil arch is a bust of an angel or saint and one female figure said to be Mary Magdalene holding a box of spikenard (an aromatic plant used for anointing) such arcading is typical of St Hugh's work (*right*).

All along this aisle can be found wonderful carvings, see if you can spot these fine examples.

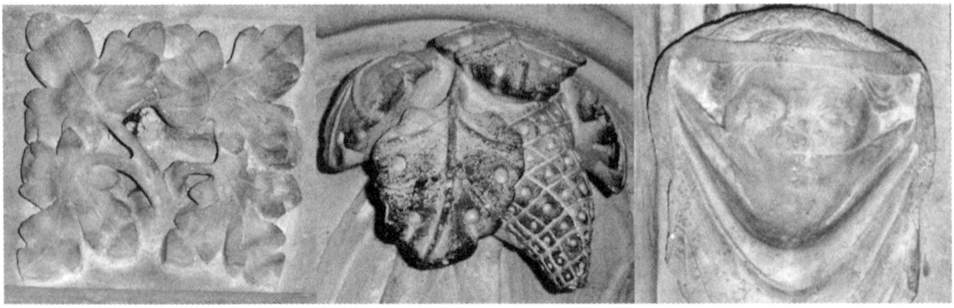

On the right as you walk down the aisle is a wall of carved flower tiles amongst which is a birds nest with two chicks inside.

It is flanked by the two parent birds.

On the opposite wall is a beautiful carved ivy ball.

Finally in this section see if you can find the dragon watching you as you pass by.

Shrine of little St Hugh

The murder of this small boy caused local uproar (See 'Jews Court' for the story). After his death the dean and chapter claimed the boy's body and he was treated like a martyr with a shrine erected. It has been much mutilated over the years. The arcade behind has five arches carved with a ball flower where traces of colouring and gilding remain.

South East transept

On the corner here notice the pillars which have what are known as 'monumental crockets'. Worth knowing just for the pleasure of being able to use the phrase which relates to hook shaped and stylised curled plant parts. They can be very ornate or quite plain like these which are unusual for being behind pillars.

In this transept you will find the Tomb of Robert Grossteste Bishop of Lincoln from 1235 to 1253. He was a huge influence on English thought and responsible for much of the cathedrals building.

Just opposite the south east transept to the right of the steps into the choir you will see Katherine Swynfords tomb which we will explore later but turn around and see if you can spot this little fellow who has been watching you!

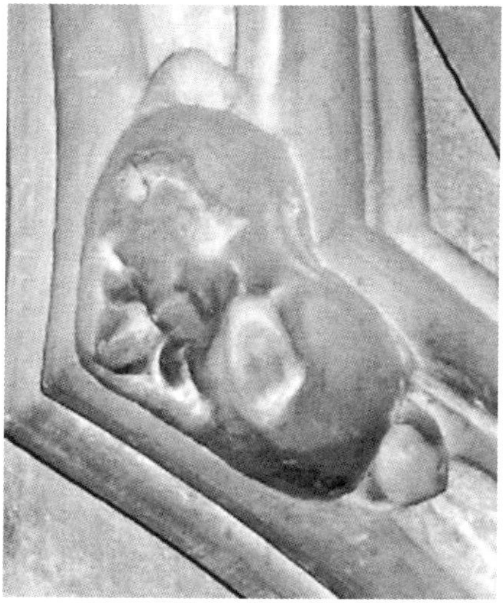

Bishop Longland's Chantry

This has some very elaborate details and over the flat archway is the inscription 'longa terra mensura eius dominus dedit' which translated is about God giving us our time on earth. Note the vines carved along the ceiling line. Longland was Bishop of Lincoln from 1521 to 1547. He entertained Henry VIII in 1541 at the Bishops Palace. Only his heart is interred here as he gave instructions for his body to be buried in a chapel at Eton and his bowels at Woburn where he died!

Bishop Russell's Chantry

Bishop John Russell was chancellor of England under Richard III and he was Bishop of Lincoln from 1480 to 1494. The bulk of the brass of the tomb was stolen like many of the others so this piece is quite a rarity.

Roof Bosses

The roof bosses here in the south aisle are worthy of note so use the

mirror provided to find the queen stroking a dog and the tree of Jesse (a man playing a harp). Your binoculars will help here too.

At the far end of the south Aisle is a quiet spot for prayer and contemplation and here you will find two heavily mutilated tombs topped with headless effigies. The head and legless one belongs to Nicholas de Cantelupe, died 1355 (*right*). He was a warrior who also founded a college of priests to celebrate mass here.

His neighbour is Prior Wimbische, died 1478 (*left*). Notice that both tombs have very elaborate and high canopies and are decorated with shields which would have been richly coloured.

Eleanor Monument

When Queen Eleanor died nearby at Harby in 1290 her body was brought to Lincoln to be embalmed and the urn containing the viscera was buried here beneath the great east window.

The subsequent Eleanor crosses were erected to mark the resting places of her body on its final journey to London. Here in the Angel Choir a marble tomb with a brass effigy was erected. The present one is a reproduction

erected by the then High Sheriff Joseph Ruston in 1891 (*above*) after the first was destroyed in 1644 in the Civil War. The gilded brass figure of the queen is a copy of that cast for her tomb in Westminster Abbey by Master William Torel.

Look out behind you for this chap too (*right*), maybe he was a stonemason!

Angel Choir

'There is no structure of modest dimensions in the whole range of gothic architecture which is more beautiful in its details or more majestic in its effects than Lincolns angel choir' (Kendrick 1908).

The choir is named after the twenty-eight carved angels between the arches.

This is St Michael weighing the souls ... the good resting gently in his lap whilst the wicked upset the scales and are falling down 'helter skelter to destruction' (Mansel Sympson) (*right*).

The one below is playing a viol and the one to its right holds up two crowns (*see bottom of previous page*).

The angel of expulsion! A rather stern looking angel with sword expelling Adam and Eve from paradise (*right*).

One holding up the sun and moon (*left*). See if you can tell what the others are doing.

East window

Lighting the Angel Choir is an elegant 60 feet high window with what is called 'bar tracery'. Such tracery is composed of thin stone elements rather than thick ones so that the glass rather than the stone dominates giving a very delicate appearance ... and letting more light in.

The great east window's images include scenes from the life of Christ and Old Testament history, note in particular Adam and Eve taking the forbidden fruit followed by the expulsion from the Garden of Eden (*see bottom of previous page*). Whilst here take the time to examine the marble pillars and look at the fossils.

The Lincoln Imp

This leering, hairy, horned, cloven hoofed, 12 inch high symbol of the City is responsible for several stories concerning his origins. It is said that the 'imp' was blown into the cathedral by strong winds and once here kept disrupting the building work of the Angel Choir. An annoyed angel threw a stone at him hitting his leg and so there he sits on the corbel nursing his sore leg (*right*)!

Another version has it that two imps were sent by the devil to make mischief after they had finished twisting Chesterfields spire and one entered the cathedral and basically ran amok throwing books and breaking candles and scaring the choirboys, etc. He then made his mistake and started to insult the angels, so an angel turned him to stone and there he sits with a mischievous grin on his face.

It is said that the passing imp was blown into the cathedral by a strong wind and the south west corner of the cathedral is still a very windy spot for some reason. A less fanciful version has it that he was deliberately carved to remind pilgrims to St Hugh's shrine of the dangers of evil. Whichever you go for, 'imp' spotting is a favourite tourist pastime here.

St Hugh's Shrine

In building the cathedral Bishop Hugh introduced elements of styles he was familiar with in France. These included tall pointed windows and slender pillars but he did not live to see it finished and died in 1200. So respected was Bishop Hugh that King John himself came to Lincoln for his burial and was a coffin bearer allegedly helping carry it up steep hill. King William of Scotland was also in attendance. In opposition to the advice of many King John insisted on wearing his crown. An ancient legend has it that ill luck will visit any monarch who enters the city walls wearing his crown.

"The first crowned head that enters
Lincolns walls,
His reign proves stormy, and his
kingdom falls"
(Boots chemist guide, 1899)

Bearing this in mind Henry II in 1167 chose to be crowned outside the city walls so as not to court disaster.

Hugh was canonised twenty years after his death and so his shrine became a place of pilgrimage. It was also known for miracles, thus drawing many to the cathedral and city along with their money and offerings. Eventually so many came that it was decided to build a better shrine to Hugh and to make room for it part of the old city walls had to be pulled down.

The shrine was consecrated and St Hughs body moved here on 6 October, 1280 prompting Kendrick (1898) to call it the 'proudest day in the history of the city'. King Edward I was in attendance with Queen Eleanor, whose own effigy was soon to lay under the same roof. Many other noble and bishops and 250 knights were in attendance at Hugh's 'enshrinement'. The shrine was ornamented with gold silver and precious stones. For some reason St Hugh's head was detached and placed in a separate coffer of silver and gold and guarded day and night. However, it was apparently stolen in 1364 for the jewels and precious metal which covered it. The head was found in a field where according to legend a crow is said to have guarded it until it was recognised and returned to Lincoln. The thieves were apprehended, hung in Lincoln and another coffer made.

St Hugh's and other shrines were ransacked in 1540 on the orders of Henry VIII who most benevolently was 'determined to bring his loving subjects to the right knowledge of the truth by taking away all occasions of idolatry' they having been 'brought into great superstition' and in need of his help. So he took away superstitious relics, superfluous plates, 4,000 ounces of silver and around 2,600 of gold, pearls, diamonds and rubies and placed them in the safe keeping of the jewel house in the Tower of London to swell his coffers (Abel and Chambers 1939). He is even said to have taken one of St Pauls teeth and one of St Catherine's fingers! ... Or so the story goes.

More damage to the cathedral was yet to come in the form of the Civil War. In 1644 Roundheads or Parliamentarians gained entry to the city and cathedral and tore brasses off tombs, stole ornaments and pictures, damaged windows and removed lead from them and the roof for bullets. It is even said that they stabled their horses inside.

In front of the shrine is a piece of the original pavement worn by the feet of many pilgrims, 'the scooped out piece of pavement in front testifies to the adoration of the many worshippers'

(Mansell Sympson). One fanciful story has it that when you close your eyes to pray here you were in danger of the devil creeping up behind you ... so the shallow dip contained salt which you could throw over your shoulder to blind the devil!

Be sure to check out the fossils in the floor too!

Table tombs

One is supposed to mark the spot of the original burial place of St Hugh and has a Latin inscription which reads ...

> *"Gold and not marble should these ashes hide,*
> *Might not some second sacrilege betide,*
> *Sad sign of a degenerate age and men,*
> *That what is marble now was silver then,*
> *With frugal Hugh well fits the humbler stone,*
> *And he who builds this tomb, prepares his own"*

Of the costly shrine which once stood here nothing remains.

Monument to Bishop Wordsworth

He was the nephew of the poet William and died in 1885. The tomb is

topped by an elaborate canopy which repays close inspection.

The base is decorated with gothic arcading and figures of the twelve apostles, so see if you can recognise any of them. Below is St Andrew (*left*) and … you decide!

And take care not to rouse the sleeping dragon at his feet!

Burghersh monuments

The first of these is to Robert Burghersh (*left*).

The next to Bishop Henry Burghersh. One time bishop of Lincoln and chancellor of England to Edward III he baptised the Black Prince but was more of a statesman than a cleric as was common in those days. His monument has a much defaced effigy, with a mitre supported by two angels. On the north side of the monument are five arches containing from the head Edward III, his four sons, Edward the Black Prince, Lionel Duke of Clarence, John of Gaunt and Edmund Duke of York. A story has it that whilst in Buckinghamshire Henry enclosed the lands of the local poor in order to extend his own parkland. His ghost could then not rest after his death and appeared in hunting dress to the canons of Lincoln beseeching them to open up his parkland and

restore the land to its rightful possessors, which they duly did.

Tomb of Lord Bartholomew Burghersh

This is a magnificent tomb. He was Henry's older brother and a soldier of much renown who fought at Crechy. His effigy is clad in armour and two angels at the head hold his family shield and two at his feet bear away in a cloth the deceased warriors soul.

The Fleming Chantrey

Richard Fleming was the founder of Lincoln college Oxford and Bishop of Lincoln from 1419. The tomb has the bishops effigy with his mitre held by two angels and his feet resting on a dragon. Underneath is a representation of his emaciated body after death such figures were common as reminders of our worldly mortality. Note the door and oak roof with vine and oak foliage.

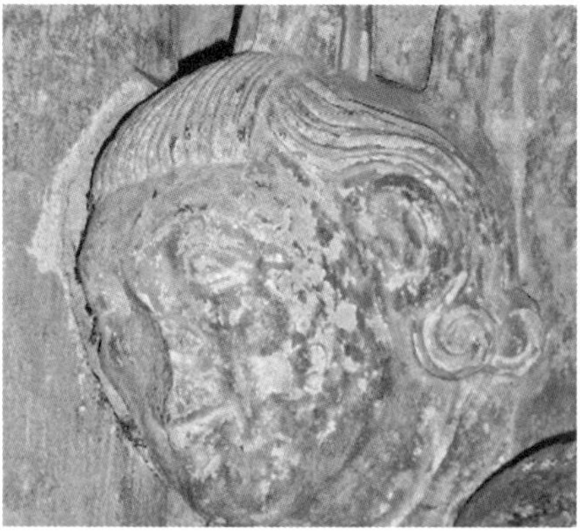

As you walk up the north aisle Note this chap next to a pillar (*left*) ... a miscalculation perhaps, as they had to cut away some of the pillar to get him in!

Down at your feet see if you can find the grave slab of Robert Dymoke of Scrivelsby, died 1735. He and many of his family held the office of Kings Champion for nearly five centuries. It was the champion's duty after a coronation to ride into the banquet in Westminster Hall in full armour and challenge to combat anyone who disputed the monarch's right to reign.

And don't forget to look above you at the splendid foliate roof bosses and one or two strangers therein!

St Hugh's Choir

This is another crowning glory of the cathedral and an orgy of superb wood

carving. St Hugh's Choir is also called the 'Crazy Vault' because of the out of kilter geometric vaulting in the ceiling. Possibly an experiment to strengthen the roof which was found to be displeasing and thus not repeated elsewhere. Some say that it looks like a bird with half folded wings. I can't see it myself … I get bats wings but look up and see what you think!

Choir stalls

You need to take your time here because the quality of the woodcarving is breathtaking, so much so that in his King's England series Lincolnshire volume Arthur Mee (1949) said, 'Altogether the stalls of Lincoln make an astonishing gallery of medieval carving, unsurpassed anywhere in the land'.

Take a look first at the canopies of the stalls.

Find the one with a statue of St Hugh with the swan. He is said to have befriended it and kept it as a pet so that it became his symbol.

Misericords

There are also many wonderful and often quirky misericords each carved from a single piece of oak. There are sixty-two in all but they are not all on display. These hinged stall seats served as supports in the long services when choristers were required to stand. It is not just the seats but the elbow rests and bench ends which are richly carved with grotesques and religious scenes by medieval artists with a sense of humour. You might find these ...

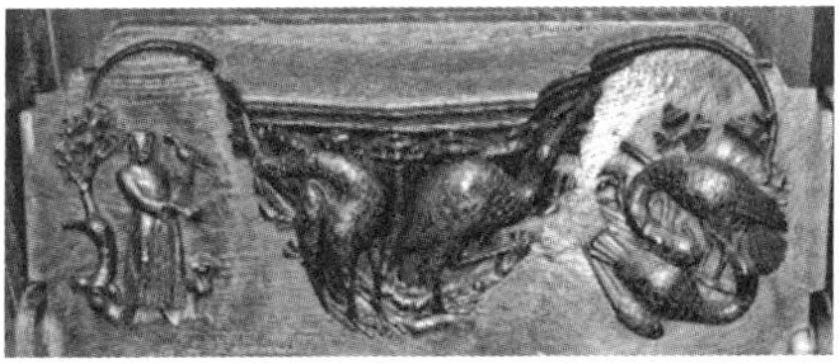

Other themes are a fox preaching to birds and then running riot amongst them. This was a common misericord theme ... the established clergy felt a lot of animosity to the new Greyfriars who came establishing their friaries amongst the monasteries and abbeys of the established church. The Greyfriars had a certain humility and affinity with the poor which almost shamed the riches and somewhat high lifestyles of the bishops and established church ... non conformists almost! Other misericords depict a man beating down acorns and pigs feeding, a mermaid with comb and mirror, a monkey riding a unicorn and a fine one of a Knight falling from his horse his armour pierced by an arrow.

Bench ends and poppy heads

Many of the bench ends and poppy heads tell stories or have elaborate and amusing designs.

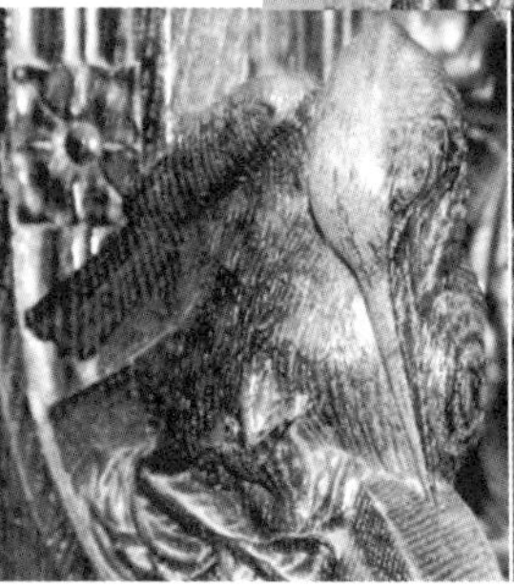

Find Delilah having cut off Samsons hair, and on the reverse is an even more severe barber with his chained victim (*below*).

The poppy head of the Precentor's reading desk tells the story of a thievish monkey stealing butter which two others have been churning and who is being hanged for his troubles.

On the bishops throne carved in 1778 notice the figures of saints and angels and just to the side this monk at prayer.

Panels

Easy to see are the many panels which again depict some strange things but are non the less superbly carved, such as this knight tilting.

And what are these up to!

Check these animals including the unusual snail and the strange frog disembowelling itself, a trio of beasts. a green man, and another imp maybe.

And introducing the band …

The pulpit dates to 1864 and is wonderfully carved so take time to look all around it and notice the elaborate canopy (*below*).

If you have not already done so then go to evensong. These services last around forty minutes and transport you back in time. You can sit on the

misericord seats in the choir stalls and listen to 16th century choral music written by the likes of William Byrd.

Katherine Swynford's tomb

This is a much mutilated tomb which has been robbed of its ornament and you can clearly see the indentations where the brasses had been. Katherine Swynford was the third wife of John of Gaunt. He married her here in the cathedral in 1396 and as Earl of Lincoln he was once possessor of the castle. He is said to have built a mansion for Katherine to the south of the city along the high street to provide a better home than the castle. John fathered four children by Katherine whilst she was his second wife's governess. He married her when his wife died. All the sovereigns of England since Henry IV are John's descendants. Opposite lies the Easter Sepulchre with its fascinating carved relief of three Knights sleeping in their chainmail.

It is a beautiful specimen of decorated work with six vaulted arches divided into two parts by a screen wall of foliage. Note the elaborate walkway above as you rejoin the North Aisle and head towards the cloisters.

Cloisters

In the passage leading to cloisters there is much carving to be seen of bosses with foliage and figures. Note too on the floor of this passage the old grave stones (*right*).

There was no need for the cloisters themselves really as it was not a monastery but they were added in 1290. Again notice the wooden roof bosses from around 1300 and look for ... a chap with a headache, a chap blowing two horns, a long eared rabbit or is it a hare?, a dog scratching, a man with toothache and various insults!

Note the old lead cast cistern in the corner with vine stems carved on it (*right*). One wonders at the prevalence of lead poisoning!

From the Doric arches of the Sir Christopher Wren designed library can be had one of the finest views of the central tower.

Along the wall see if you can find these curious creatures below.

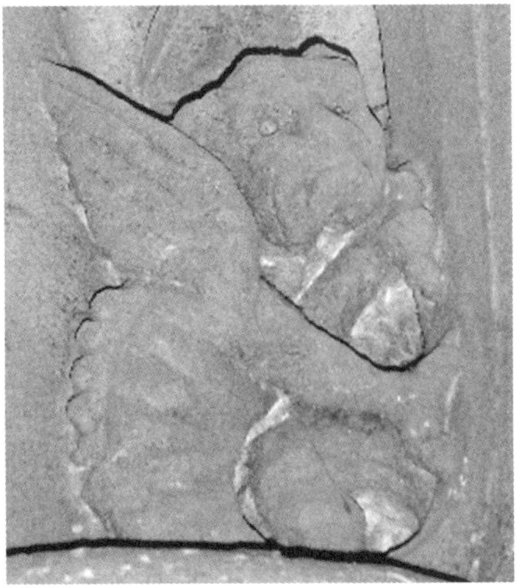

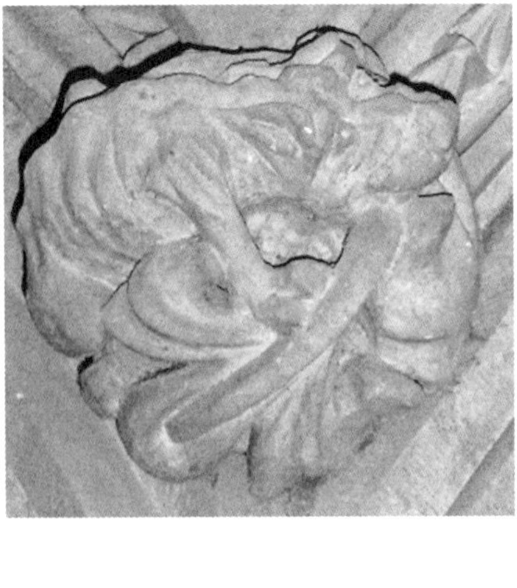

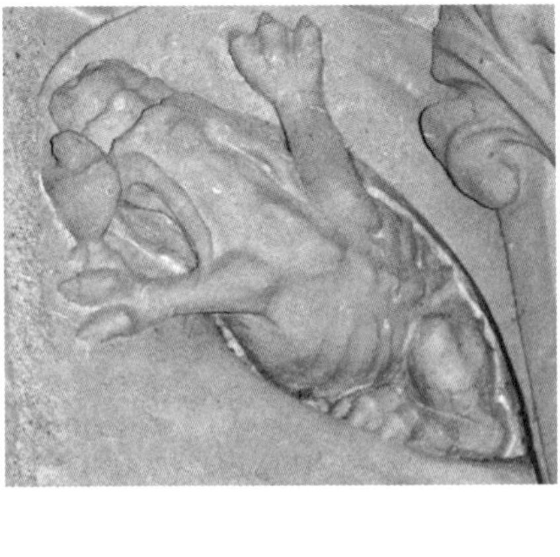

Chapter House

This was the first polygonal chapter house in England and a ten-sider at that … decagonal! Vaulting ribs are carried down to a central shaft with ten hexagonal Purbeck shafts and a rich foliated capital. The stained glass windows detail the history of the cathedral from its foundation. Look for … (*left to right from top*) the panel depicting laying the foundations, and again!, a girl meeting the king, more construction, the fire which destroyed the cathedral and St Hugh's Burial.

Cromwell's soldiers smashing the place to bits (*right*) and a visit from John Wesley (*below*).

The chapter house has seen some events in its time. When the order of the Knights Templar, the great crusaders, was suppressed by the king of France some of them were sent here to be tried in 1310. The wooden chair in chapter house with lions as arm rests was used by Edward II when he used to hold parliamentary meetings here. Of local importance, this is also where, in 1536, Henry VIII's reply to the demands of the Lincolnshire Rising were read to the rebels whom he described as the 'rude commons' of a shire that was the 'most brute and beastly' of the realm. 10,000 yellowbelly's had descended upon Lincoln to protest against Henry's pillaging of the church's wealth but troops dispersed the mob and around 100 were executed, many in Castle Square, by the tried and tested method of hanging, drawing and quartering.

On your way out be sure to notice the stunning round window.

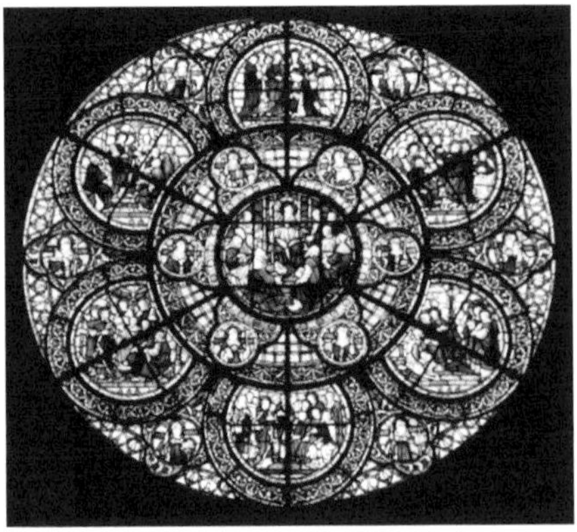

Top tip

This is a great place to come and enjoy a glass of mulled wine and mince pie during the Lincoln Christmas Market ... far from the madding crowd.

Library

Built according to Sir Christopher Wren's 'direction' the library houses a copy of the Magna Carta of which only three others exist. It was drawn up by baron, church and civic leaders who were upset at the tax situation and state of the country. They forced King John to sign it in 1215 under the threat that they would withdraw their allegiance. It was then the country's first constitution and guide to civil rights and law. The library also houses other medieval manuscripts and books printed by Caxton alongside more modern rarities such as first editions of Milton's *Paradise Lost*, Spencer's *Faerie Queene* and Cervantes' *Don Quixote.*

North aisle

Note the corbels with birds hidden in the foliage (*below, left*).

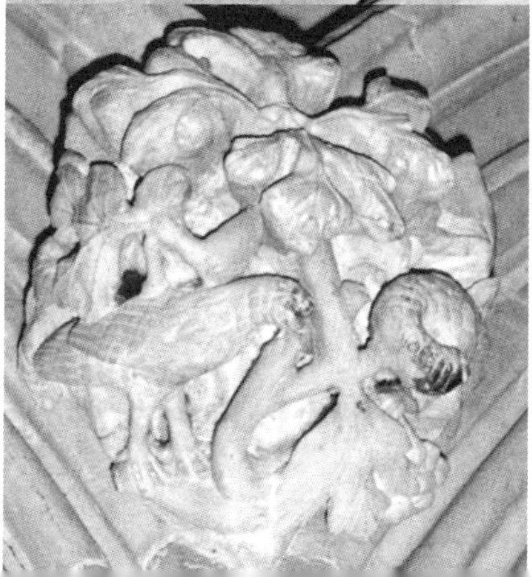

The treasury is also worth a look to see some of the fine pieces which were not looted (*below*).

North transept

Military chapels

Here is a series of three linked chapels for each of the Army, Navy and Royal Air Force. Look for these guards of honour.

And this impressive St George and the Dragon. And the model of Matthew Flinders's ship HMS investigator.

The Airforce dambusters window.

Another window depicts the nearby RAF Cranwell flying college.

Look also for the window with the aerial view of the cathedral, a sight

which returning bomber crews used to help find their way back to nearby RAF airfields.

The Dean's eye

The Dean's eye is so called as it looks out on the deanery. This 13th century Rose Window is remarkable for remaining undamaged during the civil war like most of the rest of the cathedrals stained glass. It represents the church

on earth and the church in heaven; in the centre is Christ seated in the midst of the blessed in heaven. Around are four large sections with a seemingly random selection of

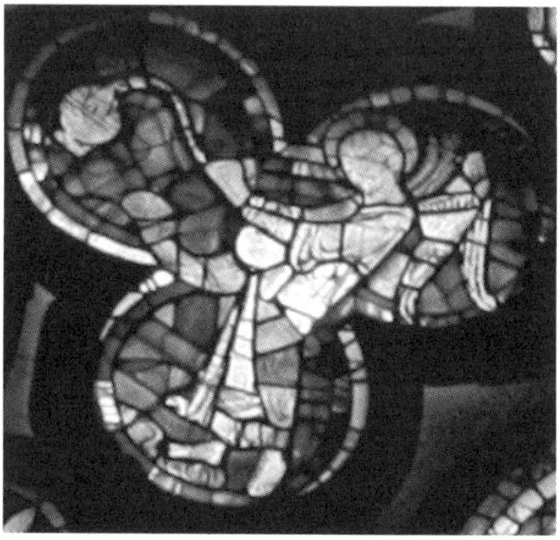

subjects. It could be that they have been rearranged over the years.

They are not easy to pick out from ground level but see if you can spot ... Christ seated on a rainbow (*top*) and the angel swinging the incense burner high (*above*).

Beneath the Deans eye and to the left check out the angel orchestra! (*left*)

Monument to William Hilton and Peter de Wint

This was erected in 1864 by Harriet de Wint, Peter's wife and William's sister. It has a lovely bas relief of one of their pictures of the cathedral, and the corner angels are superb.

Now turn back into the nave..............

Cracked tomb

Bishop Regimus used to be buried here and the site is marked by a black Tournai marble slab. This dark limestone is so hardwearing it was often used for paving slabs. Notice the crack! It is said that in the 1141 fire a blazing beam from the roof fell on it and cracked it in the middle. In detail it has a kind of sculptured tree enclosing three oval spaces of which the upper contains our Lord in glory with angels above and Moses below with Elias and horns and a fiery serpent. In the middle is a seated figure between two beasts and two angels are below this with David and his harp. Some suggest that the connection with Regimus is however unproved and at some stage the canons removed the body to a spot on the north side of the altar.

There are some excellent stained glass windows on this side of the nave in particular ... the sower window (*below left*) and the Good Samaritan (*right*).

The Teaching Window

George Boole was the founding father of computing and the digital revolution. His friends raised the money for this memorial window after he died in 1864. The central 'medallion' shows Christ teaching in the temple.

The plaque underneath sums the man up 'a man of acutest intellect ... being specially exercised in the severer sciences, dilgently explored the recesses of mathematics and happily illuminated them'. (See Silver Street)

Tours

Taking a tour with a Cathedral guide adds another dimension to your understanding and gets you some views and insights you'd otherwise miss such as ... Lucy tower from Cathedral, West Front balcony, Exchequergate (*below*),

close ups of the towers, the Sherwood Forest oak timbers holding up the roof, and a close up of Bishop Regimus in the west Front Window.

A roof tour can also give you the opportunity to see the slight miscalculation in the roofline. After the earthquake only the West Front

was left standing as it was more strongly built and fortified to encase the bishops quarters. When they rebuilt the cathedral they started at the east end and worked their way west but when they got there they were slightly out.

On leaving the Cathedral turn left towards the Bishops Palace in Minster Yard.

BISHOPS PALACE TO THE HIGH BRIDGE

Bishops Palace

Reputedly one of the best medieval buildings in the country over 800 years old. The Bishops of Lincoln were some of the most powerful people in England at one time and so could afford to build themselves a fine palace. In around 1110 Henry I granted permission for Bishop Alexander to build a dwelling on some land opposite the cathedral but he apparently never got around to it. Then in 1155 (ish) Henry II granted more land to Bishop Robert de Chesney and permission to make a doorway on the castle bailey wall to his dwelling. This gate can still be seen opposite the galilee porch which was then known as the Bishops Porch. It was later embattled and fortified with a three storey high gate tower, then were added the chapel and apartments. It was arranged in a series of terraces with what Barley (1952) called 'the finest view imaginable'. However fate dictated that it would be burnt and looted by Royalist cavaliers in the civil war and not rebuilt.

The Great Hall was started by Hugh of Avalon who died before it was finished. His successor Hugh of Wells completed it in 1234 and added a kitchen, buttery and cellars. Over the years a chapel and tower with a fine Oriel window were added, with Bishop Alnwick's coat of arms over the door.

Henry VIII was a visitor here in 1541 with Catherine Howard and Abel and Chambers (1939) tell us that the city used to make him 'lavish grants of oxen, sheep and fish'. They also made the citizens clean the streets of dung and stones and sprinkle sand along the streets for his visits. It was in this palace that the unfortunate queen was charged with having a secret 'interview' (a dangerous liason as it turned out) with Thomas Culpepper which eventually led to both losing their heads.

When here, Henry dined in the 100 foot long great hall where pillars of Purbeck marble support the roof. The hall would be hung with bright tapestries for the king's visit. Apparently the bishops had a private chamber on the first floor at the south end of the hall which had a passage leading to the kitchen!

King James I paid a visit in 1617 during which time he touched 50 people to cure them of the 'kings evil' or scrofula a swelling of the lymph nodes arising from TB. It was believed at the time that a touch from royalty could heal and the gift was said to be hereditary and proof of royalty's God given right to rule.

In 1643 it was used as a prison in the Civil War and in 1648 was set on fire by Royalists, looted and the roof stripped of its lead and left a smouldering ruin.

Much of Lincoln suffered a similar ransacking and 80 years later Daniel Defoe in his tour of England from 1722 onwards wrote that 'Lincoln was ... ancient, ragged and decayed. However it still has some beautiful ruinous architecture'.

And as with elsewhere in Lincoln you are never entirely free of scrutiny!

In the 1730s Bishop Reynolds gave permission to pull down the ruins to repair the cathedral so what we have left is but a fraction of the former palace. However it still impresses, especially with the views of the cathedral behind it.

Part of the Bishops Palace is now a hotel and within is the Ann Flinders collection. These are watercolours of flowers from nature by Ann Flinders, wife of Matthew Flinders, the Lincolnshire explorer who was the first to circumnavigate Australia and identify it as a continent. A model of his ship can be seen in the Military Chapel in the Cathedral. Notice the heraldry by the hotel entrance.

As you exit the palace notice again the Bishop Alnwick's coat of arms.

Cantelupe Chantry House

On your left here is the Precentory, originally the house of the clergy who served in the chantry founded by lord Nicholas Cantelupe. The front door seems to be protected by a happy and a not so happy cat!

Notice the fine Oriel window supported by grotesques. The shields on either side of the window are the arms of the Cantelupe and Zouche families.

Greestone Stairs

The name arises from Greeson which is early English for steps. In 1726 a mob of over 400 came through the gateway protesting against a proposal to take down the two remaining cathedral spires. Apparently they thought that the towers were going to be pulled down too! The dean and chapter had been warned that this might happen and closed the cathedral close gates. However they forgot the postern on the stairs. The story has it that the quick witted cathedral chancellor opened the beer cellars and promised the mob their views would be taken into account. Duly anaesthetised and mollified the mob withdrew. The spires did not come down until 1807. As you descend the stairs look at the fine terracotta brick work of the old Victorian Girls High School. If you feel a certain shiver as you pass the gateway half way down it is because these stairs are haunted by many ghosts. Many report a sudden strange chill as they pass through the arch at night. The most famous ghost is of a 17th century cleric who hung himself from the crooked lamppost by the archway. He is said to walk up the stairs and then disappear straight through the wall. Others just see the shadow of his body swaying on the wall. Another is of a woman carrying a baby and laying it down on a flower bed.

At the bottom of the steps turn right and enter the grounds of the Usher gallery.

Temple Gardens

These are Victorian pleasure gardens created in 1824.

Note the statues in the grounds including the sculpture *a mighty blow for freedom – XXXX the media* by M Sandle and *Mother and child* by Glynn Williams (*below*) ... take a walk around it and see how it changes!

There is also a ring sculpture in a tree commemorating the marriage between the Usher Gallery and The Collection.

The Usher Gallery

James Ward Usher was born in Lincoln on New Years Day in 1845. The son of a jeweller, he took over the family business in 1874. Their shop at

26-27 Guildhall Street was the first in the city to have electricity. Usher had a passion for the arts and collecting. His predilections included watches and enamel miniatures and these are well worth inspection. He also had a fondness for Chelsea and Worcester porcelain. He also bought the rights

to use the Lincoln Imp and made a profitable enterprise selling Imp brooches, tie pins and other souvenirs.

He was Sheriff of the city in 1916 and after his death at the age of 76 in 1921 left the city his collection along with the money to house it. His one stipulation being that the gallery bear his name. It was designed by Sir Reginald Blomfield a prolific architect who also designed the city library and the Westgate water tower and it was opened with a gold key by the Prince of Wales in 1927. Note the strange but impressive decoration on the outer walls.

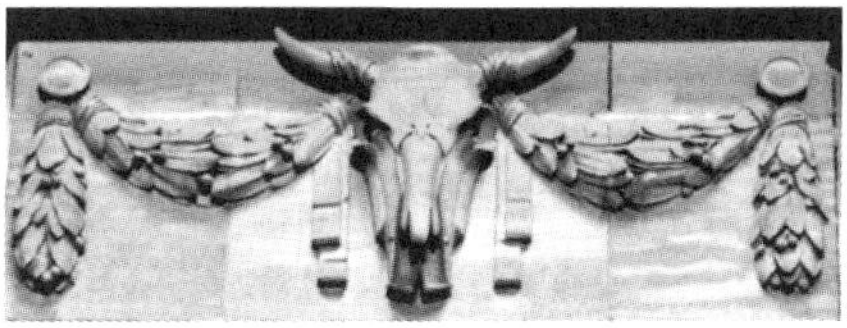

Inside are a feast of treasures and the display is fresh. It changes over time too but things to look out for include some fantastic sculpture such as *The Prodigal Son* by William Theed Junior (*below right)* and *Venus kissing Cupid* by John Gibson (*below*).

At the top of the stairs notice *Head of a sleeping child* by Thomas Wilkinson Wallis, 1862.

There is some fine pottery too, including *Fantasy Village* by Grayson

Perry, 2006, *Crab and fish saucer,* Chinese late 18th century and *Cow Creamer,* Yorkshire Prattware, 18th century (*right*).

There are many excellent paintings too including one by L S Lowry depicting the city with the foundry workers going to or from work. The collection changes from time to time but you might be lucky enough to see the following. A portrait of Tennyson's wife Emily by his friend G F Watts and a John Piper portrait of the west front of Saint Riquier church in the Somme or *The Clumber Spaniel* by George Stubbs or *Venice* by William Logsdail (*left*). This Lincoln born artist studied at the Academie Royale des beaux-Arts at Antwerp and exhibited often at the Royal Academy in London. His father was verger at the Cathedral.

'Venice' by William Logsdail © The Collection and Usher Gallery, Lincoln

Elsewhere look out for Ushers watches and miniatures such as a mandolin watch beset with jewels and another disguised as a strawberry! Paintings include works by local artist William Hilton and his friend Peter de Wint who came to love both Hilton's sister and the local landscape.

Peter de Wint

Peter De Wint was apprentice to an engraver and portrait painter in London and soon established a reputation for his drawings and watercolours. He first exhibited at the Royal Academy in 1807 and in 1809 entered the Royal Academy schools. He visited Lincoln with the painter William Hilton who was born here. He married Hilton's sister Harriet in 1810 and subsequently visited Lincoln often, painting many landscapes and rural scenes. De wint had a house near the castle but lived much of the time in London and travelled around the country sketching and painting. He ranks amongst the country's finest watercolourists and his rough field sketches capture vivid snapshots with just a few lines. It is easy to see why he was once credited with coming the nearest of any artist to painting the perfect picture.

'Lincoln from the River at Sunset' by Peter DeWint © The Collection and Usher Gallery, Lincoln

William Hilton

The Lincoln born Hilton, the son of a portrait painter, exhibited at the Royal Academy at the age of just 16. He shared the same apprenticeship with de Wint in London where they became good friends and roomed together. He was a good portraitist but also adept at large historical scenes. He too exhibited at the Royal Academy where he eventually became keeper in 1827. His 1823

Christ crowned with thorns is regarded as his masterpiece. He has many works in the Tate and his portrait of Keats hangs in National portrait Gallery.

From here cross the road to the Collection.

The Collection to the end

This is the name given to the Lincoln Museum and Usher Gallery combined. It houses exhibitions relating to many aspects of Lincolnshire history from Stone Age times through to the Romans, Vikings and Medieval periods and beyond and will help you delve deeper into many aspects of this walk. Note in particular the Iron Age boat (*right*), the Roman Legions, and the Witham shield. And don't miss the impressive bone combs.

From the collection slip down Flaxengate to Silver Street.

Silver Street

Number 34 is the birth place, in 1815, of George Boole, the mathematician to whom there is a memorial window in the cathedral. He gave us Boolean maths or logic and it is to him we must grateful for laying the ground work of computing. He taught himself to read Latin and translate Greek in his teens. He thought mathematics could help us to understand how the brain solves problems and wrote books such as *An investigation into the laws of thought.* He started his own school in Free

School Lane where the library is now and later opened a school at 3 Pottergate where there is another memorial to him. He went on to become professor of mathematics at University College Cork, a post he was given on the strength of his publications. He was given several honorary degrees and was elected to the Royal Society and achieved all this in his short life of 49 years. Shame about the lack of a blue plaque!

Retrace your steps and cross over into Free School Lane.

Drill Hall

Built for the First Lincoln Volunteer Company and opened in May 1890 complete with rifle range. Made from brick and Ancaster stone it is embattled and even has a watch tower. Inside is a large hall with a floor which was specially constructed to dampen the sound of men practicing drill. It also had a soup kitchen which was called into good service in the typhoid outbreak of 1904/5 where it also served as a hospital with over 60 beds lining the drill floor. There was also a gymnasium, an armoury which stored the battalion's arms and a magazine. The hall was the gift of local entrepreneur and former MP for the city, Joseph Ruston. His engineering company was very successful and he was known as a tough businessman. The year he gifted the drill hall his company was making around £50,000 a year but he refused his men a pay rise asking them to 'let me get bread and cheese out of my buisiness'. He was thence known as Mr Bread and Cheese and the hall referred to as 'bread and cheese hall'. However he did let them use the hall for dances.

In its later years it became a concert hall and in its time has played host to the Rolling Stones, Roy Harper, Elvis Costello, Wilco Johnson and many more.

It is now a thriving arts venue, theatre and concert hall. The Rolling Stones gig was on 31 December 1963 … almost their 400th that year! Note the face sculpture by Rick Kirby (*right*).

Opposite note the beehive on the Old Coop building (*above*). The library entrance is also noteworthy.

St Swithins church

This Ancaster and Lincoln stone church with its 197ft high spire was built around 1870/80 and designed by James Fowler of Louth and is considered to be one of his finest churches.

It is well worth walking around to check out the grotesques. And the rather scary humans!

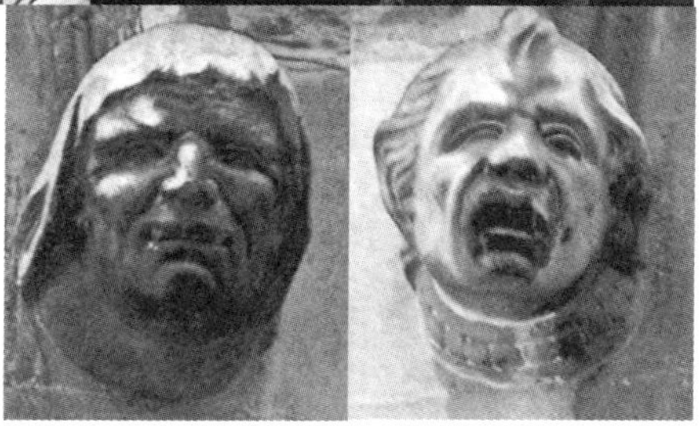

Note too the fine turrets, and the foundation stone.

A Roman altar carved on each side with sacrificial figures and cut out of solid block of Oolite, a form of limestone, was found here when they excavated the foundations. Two former St Swithins stood opposite where the graveyard and green is now and it is said that Cromwell's Parliamentarians stored gunpowder here in 1664 as they routed the city. This exploded and burnt the church down.

Over the road from the church is St Swithins vestry hall, built 1888 and now a useful café.

It has a fine doorway with angels carved in relief (*right*).

In the square there also used to be the Central Hall and Lawson Institute this used to be a lecture hall cum theatre and temperance hall. It was later converted to a cinema and the first talking film in Lincoln was shown here. It was destroyed by fire in 1944. Now sadly demolished.

Greyfriars

Between St Swithin's and the library is Greyfriars. This is the first friary founded in 1230 in Lincoln by Franciscans or Greyfriars and is the earliest in England if not Europe. Sworn to utter poverty it is no wonder the established clergy took a dislike to them. They provided an unhealthy contrast to the excesses of the bishops and clergy up at the cathedral with their palaces and long history of pub ownership. They lived on gifts made to them in return for services. They were very successful in Lincoln so much so that their expanding precinct encroached upon the city wall and ran from Silver Street to the Witham, much of its foundations now lying under the library.

This used to be the city museum from 1907 and it has a stone undercroft 100 foot long supported by superb pillars and vaulting. From the time of Henry VIII until then Victorian age it was a school hence 'Free School Lane' but it was also, at one time, a house of correction and a gunpowder store. Note the 'fish' shaped window in the east wall.

From here go up Broadgate a little way to examine the original main entrance to the Drill Hall.

The gateway has the Royal Arms carved in stone above it so look up to notice this and the fine towers.

From here go onto Broadgate and cross the river Witham and follow it back towards the High Bridge. As you

get to the square you will see the market. There was a separate butter market much further down the high street years ago and the façade of the old butter market was saved and reused here. Note the coat of arms.

From the bridge here is a fine view of your route back to the High Bridge and the end of your walk.

And here's a reminder of how it used to look.

REFERENCES AND SOURCES

Abell E and Chambers J. 1939. *The Story of Lincoln.* Lincoln. City of Lincoln Education Committee.

Barley M. W. 1952. *Lincolnshire and the Fens.* London; Batsford.

Defoe D. 1724-6. *A tour through the whole island of Great Britain.* Harmondsworth. Penguin.

Elvin L. 1974. *Lincoln as it was.* Nelson, Lancashire. Hendon publishing.

AF 1899 *Guide to Lincoln.* Lincoln. Boots cash chemists.

Golding W 1964. *The Spire.* London. Faber and Faber. This will give you an insight into the building of a medieval cathedral.

Kendrick A F. 1898. *The Cathedral Church of Lincoln; A History and Description of its Fabric and a List of the Bishops.* London. George Bell and Sons

Mansell Sympson E. 1906. *Lincoln; A historical and topographical account of the city.* London. Methuen.

Marsden W. 1977. *Lincolnshire.* London. Batsford.

Mee A. 1949. *The King's England; Lincolnshire.* London. Hodder and Stoughton.

Melton L. M. Undated. *One hundred and fifty years at the lawn.* No named publisher.

Morton H. V. 1929. *The Land of the Vikings.* Bungay. The Chaucer Press.

Srawley J. H. Rev. 1947. *The Story of Lincoln Minster.* London. Raphael Tuck and Sons.

Yates J. and Thorold H. 1965. *Lincolnshire; A Shell Guide.* London. Faber and Faber.

Yeates-Langley A. 2009. 'The Lincoln House of Industry' and 'The Union workhouse' in *Uphill Lincoln 1: Burton Road, Newport and the Ermine Estate.* Ed A Walker. Published by The Survey of Lincoln.

Useful web sites

www.countyassemblyrooms.co.uk/history
www.wattsgallery.org.uk/picture-focus/monument-tennyson

https://archive.org/stream/lifeofsthughofav00perruoft/lifeofsthughofav00perruoft_djvu.txt

This will take you to a life of St Hugh. See appendix E for a list of miracles attributed to St Hugh. They are a fascinating glimpse into the world at that time.